Chicago Catholic Women:
Its Role in Founding
the Catholic
Women's Movement

—❀❀❀—

Donna Quinn

Chicago Catholic Women:
Its Role in Founding the Catholic Women's Movement
Donna Quinn

Distributed by:

Lake Claremont Press: A Chicago Joint, an imprint of Everything Goes Media, LLC
www.lakeclaremont.com
www.everythinggoesmedia.com

20 19 18 17 16   10 9 8 7 6 5 4 3 2 1

Production by Conspire Creative (*www.conspirecreative.com*) is dedicated to Darlene Noesen and in memory of Joanne Cullen. Design work by Todd Petersen.

Printed in the United States of America.

*To all the women and men of Chicago Catholic Women
and to my family—
especially my mother; my father; my brother, Bill; my sister, Joyce;
and to all who have gone before us.*

CONTENTS

PREFACE

I wrote this book for several reasons.

- To give it as a gift to women and men, now and in the future, so that they will know what was done for them by women and men who were committed to working for their full equality in the Church and in societies of the global community.
- To write the *herstory* of Chicago Catholic Women so that our role in one of the greatest movements of the twentieth century—the Women's Movement—might be known and celebrated.
- To show the importance of Chicago Catholic Women as one of the founders of the Catholic Women's Movement.
- To lift up the strength, courage, and perseverance of great women who planted the seeds of justice in a church that never appreciated their giftedness, and in a world that continues to oppress women and our daughters.

This herstory of Chicago Catholic Women is one that Chicago can be proud of, and one that began many of the groups, coalitions, and organizations that continue to work for the elimination of gender discrimination.

Intertwined with this herstory of Chicago Catholic Women are my brief reflections and recollections of the people and happenings that informed my life, and gave me the courage to continue my work. I am so grateful for them and for my family, who is rooted in Chicago.

I am a firm believer that life can be looked at in 25-year spans, and from there we can listen again to the Spirit within to direct us to create the "new." The 25-year span of this wonderful organization called Chicago Catholic Women presents us with this herstory and memoirs.

CHAPTER 1
Finding Courage and Strength from Those Who Have Gone Before Us

The rain fell gently on eight cousins huddled under umbrellas at the grave of their grandmother who had died 80 years earlier on this very day. This day was planned to honor a strong woman named Ann, who with her husband, Joe, and the last of their children, came to the U.S. from Limerick, Ireland. While seven older children were waiting in Chicago for their arrival, Joe—with twins Kathleen and Gerry, and the youngest, my dad, Bill—was dealing with the heart attack and death of his wife, Ann, as the ship approached New York Harbor and Ellis Island. My grandmother had managed to get her family to the U.S. but she died on the boat before entering the harbor. Now 80 years later, her spirit was with her granddaughters: Terese O'Keefe, Ruth Vaulman, Joan Kelly, Ruth Pauly, Marge Quinn, Marilyn Quinn, Anne Kempton, and myself, Donna Quinn—eight women who knew her only through family stories and honored her strength and determination.

–❀❀❀–

I was born and raised Catholic on the South Side of Chicago. I would always rattle it off with the identifying attributes for me: Feminist, Irish, Catholic, Democrat, Chicagoan, and White Sox fan.

Being Catholic was so much a part of who I was. I had watched altar boys on the altar at daily mass in grade school at St. Gabriel parish and wondered why I couldn't do that. I remember when I was in first grade, an uncle asked me at a family gathering if I wanted to be a nun and I said, "No, I want to be a Sister." (I was not familiar with the term *nun*.) And now I say, *we are all Sisters in the Movement.*

In seventh grade, an order priest came to our classroom and told us about his life as a priest. I was very taken with his words and before he left he asked, "Who would like to be a priest?" My hand shot up. The boys in the room laughed. The priest smiled and said, "No, that is not possible for girls."

My whole family was parish and Church oriented. My father helped to run the parish fundraisers at the Palmer House downtown. He was one of the head ushers and president of the Holy Name Society and St. Vincent de Paul Society, which worked for the poor of our parish, gathering food and clothing for them. We never knew which families he and the other men were helping. This was always confidential.

Everyone loved my mother. They liked talking and laughing with her, especially the young adults who were on their way to, or just coming back from, WWII. They thought she was a "with it" person with whom they could identify. I watched my mother roller skate on our block and turn on the "pump" (fire hydrant) so that the neighborhood kids might get some relief from the summer heat.

My sister, Joyce, was president of her class in high school. She used to say that she spent her grade school days tutoring the kids who needed extra help. I believe that began her love of teaching in grade and high school and why so many of the . "outcasts" would gather in her art room after school for a safe place to talk and laugh with her and with each other.

I always prayed that my brother, Bill, would be a good, holy parish priest, and those prayers were positively answered. He was the steady rock upon whom I rested.

—❀❀❀—

In addition to the inspirations of my family, I prepared for this writing by drawing inspiration from others who have gone before us. I started by visiting with Margaret Traxler in Mankato, MN. A stroke took Margaret's ability to vocally articulate but her eyes and spirit would not be silenced. Margaret, from her wheelchair, held our hands tightly as the National Coalition of American Nuns blessed her during our celebration of the Eucharist together.

My next trip planned would look to three women buried in the Seneca Falls–Rochester, New York, area for inspiration. Two of the women, Susan B. Anthony (1820–1906) and Elizabeth Cady Stanton (1815–1902), were responsible for the first women's meeting that was held in Seneca Falls in 1848. They listed the rights they demanded: to vote, to be educated, to enter any occupation, to have control over their bodies, to sign legal papers, to manage their own earnings, and to administer their own property.[1] Anthony traveled out West many times speaking out for the right of women to vote. By 1893, at the Columbian Exposition in Chicago, with Susan B. Anthony as speaker, a World Council of Women convened, inaugurating an international feminist movement. It wasn't until after their deaths that the Nineteenth Amendment passed (1920), giving women the right to vote. The third woman was Harriet Tubman (1826–1913), who helped establish the "underground railroad" leading people from slavery to freedom, and who later helped organize the National Federation of Afro-American Women in 1895.

My cousin Ginger Krabbe was to go to Seneca Falls–Rochester with me, but our travel plans were cut short by the closing of airports after September 11, 2001. This trip would have to wait for a later date, but the spirit of these women remains a guiding light.

– ❁❁❁ –

In the early days of the movement, I sincerely believed that the Catholic Church was *my* Church. How many times the media asked me why I stayed and wouldn't it be easier just to leave it! I would always respond that this was my Church and I loved it. Where would I go? Those words of Peter answering Jesus kept coming back to me (John 6:67–68). Changing religious communities or changing denominations to be ordained never made sense to me. It was never the ordination itself, but rather, the struggle to allow all women to be ordained in the Catholic tradition that propelled me forward.

---

1   Judy Chicago, *The Dinner Party* (New York: Anchor Books, 1979), 89.

CHAPTER 2

The Founding of Chicago Catholic Women: Born of Inspiration, Vision, and Necessity

On August 5, 1974, I arrived at St. Thomas the Apostle High School in Chicago to start the next chapter in my life. At St. Thomas, I would teach religion, math, and history to young women in high school and work with the community and parents in development work. This was my first assignment in Chicago, bringing me back home after fifteen years away. Prior to this, I taught sixth, seventh, and eighth grades, as well as high school, for 15 years in Nebraska, Illinois, Minnesota, and Wisconsin. During the sixties, I had worked on racial issues in parishes and now, in the seventies, I felt an excitement for the emerging Women's Movement building within me.

On Monday, October 14, 1974, the Association of Chicago Priests held a conference called "Ministry on the Upturn" at the Lutheran School of Theology in Hyde Park, a neighborhood on the South Side of Chicago. The workshops began at 3:30 p.m. with an opening address by Monsignor John Egan. According to the brochure, the conference was "based on Christian Hope," with an emphasis on "effective ministry going on now." The brochure also stated that "many of these workshops are of interest to all the people of God, not only priests." Each workshop consisted of input by those engaged in ministry work, followed by feedback and sharing.

The topics to be covered in this one-day workshop were listed as "Sharing, Community, Support, Charism, Initiative, Encouragement, Healing, Freedom, and Ideas." There were thirteen workshops in all: Apostolate to the Deaf, Christian Dignity: Ministry to Gay Catholics, Pastoral Care Today: A Model, Danced Prayer, Deacon Internship Program: St. Mary of the Lake Seminary, Parish Staff Teamwork, Pentecostal Community, Permanent Deaconate, Red Is Dead, Significant Liturgies, Sisters in Parish Ministries, Suburban Community, and Youth Prayer Groups.

Before coming to Chicago I was offered the ministry of working with the Deaconate Program in Milwaukee; that would have changed my life. I also went out to Los Angeles to look at working in Development for Religious Communities; that, too, would have changed my life. Now, looking back, I can say that the "Ministry on the Upturn" workshops sponsored by the Association of Chicago Priests that October afternoon changed my life.

It was a crisp, sunny autumn day as I left my classroom and walked across Woodlawn Avenue for the start of the conference. Unaware what a turning point it would be for me, I was on my way to the 4 p.m. "Sisters in Parish Ministry" workshop because of the woman leading the session. I was missing the strong women's group I had left in Milwaukee, and Marge Tuite was a well-known progressive activist with a huge presence. My second choice for workshops was "Red Is Dead" because I wanted to learn more about the racist practice of redlining homes for sale in Chicago.

The room filled up quickly with nuns from everywhere in the city to hear Sr. Cyrilla Zarek from Mercy Hospital, Sr. Joanne Seiser from Circle Campus Ministry, Sr. Carlotta Oberzut from St. James Parish, Sr. Marita Enright from the CCD-Team Retreats, Sr. Mary Priniski from Ford City, and Sr. Marjorie Tuite, facilitator of the panel.

Later when the discussion was underway, I raised my hand and asked, "Where is the women's group in Chicago?" I gave my name, told the room I was new in Chicago and that I hadn't found a women's group to join, and asked *didn't we need one in this big city?* A woman two rows ahead of me turned her head quickly and said she agreed with me. (I later found out that her name was Sr. Gabriel Herbers or Gabe, as she was known). Heads started nodding "Yes" and soon the discussion centered on the need for such an organization. The workshop concluded and Marge Tuite came up to me with her New York accent and said, "If you get a women's group started, I will help you in whatever way I can."

— ❀❀❀ —

Chicago, the largest Archdiocese in the Church, was teeming with social justice activists in the sixties and early seventies, many of whom were 10 to 20 years older than I was at the time. To them, this new Women's Movement seemed different than the justice issues they had worked on in the sixties—peace, labor issues, race relations, marriage issues, and implementing Vatican

II. They didn't seem to understand the Women's Movement and what this feminism was all about. Or, if they did, they weren't sure that we, the younger generation, could really pull it off. We didn't realize when we came on the Chicago scene in the seventies that this Women's Movement would later be recognized as one of the most important movements of the twentieth century.

Social justice activists came through the sixties supporting the Civil Rights Movement. While we preached and believed in equality, we knew by the seventies that this was still lacking for women, not only in society, but more specific to our concerns, in the Church. Vatican II, the Vietnam War, and the Civil Rights Movement raised liberation consciousness, but women would yet have to organize on behalf of their own equality.

Nuns became involved in social justice organizing. The National Assembly of Women Religious (NAWR), which began in 1968, and the National Coalition of American Nuns (NCAN), founded in 1969, put forth agendas relating to such issues. In 1976 at the NAWR meeting in Nazareth, KY, the House of Delegates passed a resolution supporting the rights of employees in Catholic institutions (mainly schools and hospitals) to organize for collective bargaining. Kathleen Keating, NAWR chairperson, urged those hesitating in their support by stating that she didn't buy the fact that unions would come in and destroy the schools; the resolution did pass by a narrow margin. The process used was a free-form one of consensus, now used in many religious communities.

New lifestyle options were emerging for nuns in this era. While Marjorie Tuite, a member of the ministerial team at the Jesuit School of Theology in Chicago and facilitator of this Kentucky NAWR meeting, indicated an unwillingness among delegates "to say any one lifestyle is the way to go in the eighties," Kathleen Keating stated that the "common denominator would be simplicity." As the team considered external and internal questions, Arlene Swidler, a participant, suggested that the nuns look at the absence of justice demonstrated by the prevailing assumption that sisters had more credibility than laywomen.

NAWR supported the United Farm Workers. They urged their membership to seek out solutions surrounding abortion (Roe v. Wade passed in 1973). They voted against the death penalty and war. They supported the National Conference of Catholic Bishops' Bicentennial Program. They used bread and wine at their own women-led Eucharistic liturgies. Even with this work on social justice issues, NAWR membership was slipping by 1976—down about 20 percent since its beginning just eight years earlier.

While NAWR was inspired by nuns like Anita Caspary (formerly Mother Humiliata of the Immaculate Heart of Mary Sisters of Los Angeles) and Mary Reilly (a sister of Mercy), NCAN received its inspiration from Margaret Traxler, a School Sister of Notre Dame. Margaret reached out to Church Women United, a coordinating group of Protestant and Eastern Orthodox women, and to the American Jewish Committee. Seminars were held in Cleveland, Pittsburgh, and Milwaukee under the banner "Institute of Women Today." Margaret's sassy remarks were quoted, "It is deplorable that religions, as interpreted by men, subjugate women in the name of the deity. To do wrong is one thing. To do wrong in the name of the Almighty is especially heinous.... We have a duty as women, as good Pope John XXIII said, to demand our equal rights. Nothing less can be in the mind of God."[2]

— ❀❀❀ —

Chicago's progress was not helped by the arrival of a man named John Cody. Cardinal John Cody was born in St. Louis, December 24, 1907. He had been Bishop of St. Louis, 1947–1956; Bishop of Kansas City, 1956–1961; and Bishop of New Orleans, 1961–1964. He was appointed Archbishop of Chicago in 1965, made a Cardinal in 1967, and died in 1982. During his years in Chicago, he lacked the ability to communicate with and trust the decisions made by priests, nuns, and other laity. Ed Dufficy of St. Francis Cabrini Church, and spokesperson for 11 West Side parishes, said that priests had been unable to meet with Cody on any issues. "When we write to the Cardinal we get a reply from Monsignor Francis Brackin (Vicar General for Administrative Affairs) who says he will meet with us. The Cardinal is isolating himself from the Archdiocese."[3]

The Association of Chicago Priests began in 1966 as priests in the Archdiocese saw the need to come together for support and discussion about issues of concern to them, as they witnessed a bishop who began to shut them out of consultation. Cody's attitude, they declared, "has resulted in a tragic waste

2   Irving Spiegel, "Women to Review Roles in Religion," *The New York Times*, 25 October, 1974.
3   Jerry DeMuth, "Chicago: Anguished Clergy, Poor," *National Catholic Reporter* Vol. 11, No. 39 (September 5, 1975): 1, 20.

of energy and talent by people on all levels in the Archdiocese of Chicago."[4] Ironically, Cody endorsed this new organization at their first gathering on May 24, 1966, at McCormick Place.

The Priests Senate, which began in 1970, also felt their lack of involvement in any decision-making. Burning issues were subsidies to parishes in need and school closings. Andrew Greeley—at that time, Director of the Center for the Study of American Pluralism at the National Opinion Research Center—explained that the tension was really "about the whole nature of the structure of the Church and the credibility of Church leadership...." Anyone who is interested in the fate of the Catholic Church in the United States, Greeley observed, "should keep an eye on Chicago."[5]

1974 marked eight years of turmoil and frustration with Cardinal Cody by local priests. If the priests thought their voices were not heard by the Cardinal, you can only imagine how women felt about our likelihood to impact the Church in the Chicago Archdiocese.

—❀❀❀—

I met many people that October evening at the Ministry on the Upturn Conference and barely remember what was said at dinner and the "Red Is Dead" workshop. I do remember that we, as women, had a cause to which I now felt I would give myself totally—even given the fact that I taught full-time; did

---

4   Ibid.
5   Ibid.

development work for the high school, which meant meeting with parents and residents of Hyde Park; and had also signed up for, and was involved in, a course at the Jesuit School of Theology on Death and Dying. Even with those "givens," I was being called to a new beginning. Everything seemed new and exciting, and most of all I was young. I could do a million things at one time—well, maybe only a thousand. The greatest thought of all was that together we would change the Church in five, well, maybe 10 years. Fifteen at the most! And don't say 20 years. That was too far away and that kind of caution was for old people...

And so, Chicago Catholic Women came on the scene in 1974, born of inspiration, vision, and necessity.

Our emerging activism was being felt almost immediately. While the Chicago Archdiocesan newspaper printed an editorial disparaging attempts made by women to organize so their voices would be heard, the independent and progressive *National Catholic Reporter* quoted me on the matter in 1975, "I see a lot of hope and unity. I see a day of reckoning coming."[6]

---

6   Ibid.

CHAPTER 3

CCW's Participation in the National Conference of Catholic Bishops' Bicentennial Program

At the very end of his life Monsignor Jack Egan, a human rights activist, gave credence to the work that women had done and continue to do for the Church. His statement before his death on May 19, 2001: "I am 84 years of age, and have served the Catholic Church and the Chicago Archdiocese for 66 years.... I worked in marriage education, in ecumenical affairs, in race relations, in social justice, in community organizing, and as a pastor.... Now at this late point in life, I look at my Church and I am troubled. I see a great incongruity, and I feel I must speak out. Why are we not using to the fullest the gifts and talents of women, who constitute the majority of our membership throughout the world? I have come to believe the Church must consider the ordaining of women as priests. At 84 I have to ask our Church to open its eyes and lift its voice on behalf of another justice issue—the Church's commitment to the inclusion of women in positions of leadership and authority in the Church, including further study and discussion of the ordination of women."[7]

The words "inclusion of women in positions of leadership and

---

7   Msgr. John J. Egan, "Use the Gifts God Gives," *Corpus Reports* Vol. 27, No. 4 (July/August 2001): 24–25.

authority in the Church, including further study and discussion of the ordination of women" sounded so familiar. That's because they were the words we used *25 years earlier* in 1976 when we presented our resolutions to the Bishops' Bicentennial Conference. This conference, titled "Liberty and Justice for All—A Call to Action," was sponsored by the National Conference of Catholic Bishops (NCCB) to celebrate the United Stated Bicentennial. The conference gathered resolutions from across the United States during 1975 to be voted on by delegates at the culminating conference held in Detroit in 1976.

It was around this very Bicentennial process that Chicago Catholic Women first rallied, with the organizing support of Terri Grasso, Jeanne Stroh, and Mary Sullivan.

—✤✤✤—

After the initial inspiration at the Ministry on the Upturn conference on October 14, 1974, for an organization of women, followed by a rally to support the Urban Apostolate of Sisters (an organization funded by the Archdiocese that worked on urban issues), the focus of our emerging organization had moved quickly to a press release from Rev. James Roache, Secretary of Communications for the Archdiocese of Chicago.

Rev. Roache wrote about the Archdiocese's participation in the nationwide observance of the United States Bicentennial in 1976. Dated September 9, 1974, the press release stated that the Archdiocese "has established liaison with the Illinois Bicentennial Commission, the American Revolution Bicentennial Commission, and the National Conference of Catholic Bishops Committee for the Bicentennial."[8] Roache's statement noted Reverend Monsignor Francis A. Brackin, Vicar General, as Archdiocesan Coordinator, and Cardinal Cody, as honorary chairman, of the NCCB Committee. The following men were also named to the committee:

- Rev. Robert Clark, Superintendent, Archdiocesan School Board
- Rev. Daniel Coughlin, Director, Office of Divine Worship
- Mr. Frank Daily, President of Holy Name Societies
- Rev. Robert Festle, Director, Propagation of the Faith
- Rev. Harry Koenig, Director, Cardinal Stritch Retreat House
- Rev. William Lion, Executive Director, Illinois Catholic Conference
- Rev. Timothy Lyne, Rector of Holy Name Cathedral
- Rev. Wenceslaus Madaj, Archdiocesan Archivist
- Rev. William Madden, S.J., Archivist
- Very Rev. Thomas Murphy, Rector, St. Mary of the Lake Seminary
- Rev. James Murtaugh, Moderator, Archdiocesan Council of Catholic Women
- Rev. Msgr. John O'Donnell, Rector, Quigley Preparatory Seminary (North)

8　Rev. James P. Roache, Secretary of Communications, Archdiocese of Chicago, Media Release, 9 September 1974.

- Rev. Raymond Pavis, Director, Catholic Youth Organization
- Rev. James Roache, Secretary of Communications
- Mr. Daniel Ryan, former Secretary to Cardinal Cody
- Rev. Jerome S. Siwek, Associate Pastor, St. Constance Church
-

And so was one woman:

- Mrs. Neal Rohr, President of the Archdiocesan Council of Catholic Women

That's a total of 16 priests, two laymen, one laywoman, and zero nuns.

On January 20, 1975, a letter went to Monsignor Francis Brackin and members of the Archdiocesan Bicentennial Committee from an ad hoc committee of women religious requesting that "as Sisters working in the Archdiocese of Chicago we are requesting membership on the Archdiocesan Bicentennial Committee, which was drawing up plans under the theme 'Peace through Justice.'" We further stated that "because of our long years of service to the people of Chicago, we would like a Committee of Sisters to represent our endeavors during the last century and a half in the Archdiocese of Chicago. We trust that the present Archdiocesan Bicentennial Committee will be able to expand its membership to include Women Religious of the Archdiocese who have been chosen by the following organizations:

- Leadership Conference of Women Religious

- National Assembly of Women Religious
- Sisters Committee on Retirement Education
- Network
- Sisters Advisory Council
- Urban Apostolate of Sisters
- 8th Day Center for Justice"[9]

I signed the letter *Sister Donna Quinn, O.P., for the Ad Hoc Committee of Women Religious for the Archdiocesan Bicentennial Plan.* I carbon-copied several women religious, including Sister Mary Inviolata, R.S.M.—LCWR; Sister Susan Weeks, O.P.—NAWR; Sister Margaret Brinkman, SSND—SCORE; Sister Beth Wagner, I.H.M.—NETWORK; Sister Bernadette Eaton, C.S.J.—SAC; Sister Jeanne Stroh, S.R.—UAS; and Sister Joanne Crowley, B.V.M.—8th Day Center for Justice.

After waiting in vain for a written response, I decided to place a follow-up call to Monsignor Brackin. He told me that nuns would be represented by a Jesuit named William Madden, S.J., on the Bicentennial Committee. As you can imagine, we were not satisfied with this answer.

—✿✿✿—

At this point in our history, only nuns had robust networks and organizations working for justice in the Church. The only

---

9   Sr. Donna Quinn, O.P., Letter to Rev. Msgr. Francis A. Brackin and members of the Archdiocesan Bicentennial Committee from an ad hoc committee of women religious, 29 January 1975.

strong group at this time for laywomen was the National Council of Catholic Women (NCCW), whose membership was supported by diocesan chapters under the leadership of a male priest moderator, appointed by the bishop of that diocese. Chicago Catholic Women was the first organization to welcome and include both laywomen and nuns. It was always a burning desire of mine that all women—those who were nuns and those who were laywomen—work together, and CCW reflected that.

One woman, Rosalie Muschal-Reinhardt, can attest to that as she played a pioneering role for us in this regard. Rosalie came to Chicago from Rochester, NY, with her husband and four children in August 1974. She had studied theology at Colgate-Rochester Divinity School. Rather than accept an M.A. degree in Christian Education from there, she was told instead to go for a Masters of Divinity (M.Div.) degree as she was "priestly material." It would also save her time and money not to start over for another degree. So when she and her family moved to Chicago, she enrolled as a candidate in the M.Div. Program at the Jesuit School of Theology Chicago (JSTC). She always reminded me that, after we met in March 1975, I would ask her to come to this meeting or that meeting so that we would always have at least one laywoman represented and telling her story. When Rosalie completed her program on February 14, 1977, she was the first married woman in the U.S. to receive a M.Div. degree.

Gradually the number of laywomen in CCW began to grow. It now included women who had left religious communities for various reasons in the late sixties and early seventies. In these beginning days though, nuns far exceeded the number of lay-women at our gatherings.

$$-\text{❀❀❀}-$$

From December 1974 to February 1975, women organized under the name Chicago Catholic Women began to plan meetings with the intent of getting our justice issues recognized in the Bicentennial Program of the NCCB. Forty women met at a meeting held on February 27, 1975, and unanimously approved the following:

> Whereas we are Catholic women of the Archdiocese of Chicago with deep concern about the quality of the life and ministry of the Church, we hereby initiate a process for wide participation of Catholic women in the program of the National Conference of Catholic Bishops for the Bicentennial.

- This process will begin with a provision for gathering testimony from women regarding their experience of, and hopes for, the Church;
- Such testimony to be presented at a public hearing in the Archdiocese to which members of the Church will be invited and further,
- To be submitted to the St. Paul Regional Hearing of the NCCB Bicentennial Program in June 1975, to be incorporated into the written record.

On March 13, 1975, a steering committee gathered. We were the first board of Chicago Catholic Women: Ellen Carroll, Carol Crepeau, Terri Grasso, Georgia Mae Horrell, Joan Krebs, Lois McGovern, Mary Lou Mrozynski, Mary Sullivan, Marge Tuite, Katherine Ward, and Susan Weeks. I served as Executive Director.

In April 1975, the newsletter of the Urban Apostolate of the Sisters called *Encounter UAS* brought attention to our existence, "In the Archdiocese of Chicago a strong and growing group of women, Chicago Catholic Women, is organizing around this important Bicentennial Program. In all of history, our time, this year, is unique."[10]

—❈❈❈—

As part of their Liberty and Justice for All—A Call to Action program, the U.S. bishops called for six regional hearings throughout the U.S. during 1975:

Feb. 3–5	Washington, D.C.
April 3–5	San Antonio, TX
June 12–14	St. Paul, MN
Aug. 7–9	Atlanta, GA
Oct. 2–4	Sacramento, CA
Dec. 4–6	Newark, NJ

Working papers were written after these hearings under the

10 Urban Apostalate of Sisters, *Encounter UAS* Vol. 11, No. 7 (April 1975): 2.

topics: Church, Nationhood, Family, Personhood, Neighborhood, Ethnicity/Race, Humankind, and Work.

The results of these written records would the basis for the "National Conference on Liberty and Justice" to be held in Detroit, October 21–23, 1976. From this conference a five-year plan of implementation was expected. After Detroit and before the bishops' next meeting in May 1977, the Administrative Committee of the NCCB would prepare a statement that included historical background, the analysis of the Detroit conference, and recommendations for planning pastoral strategies for the next five years in the American Catholic Church. This was an important part of envisioning the future, and we intended to influence it and make our contribution.

At the same time, Pope Paul VI (1963–Dec. 8, 1978) declared 1975 a Holy Year of Reconciliation, and the U.N. declared 1975 International Women's Year. Women in Chicago were energized by the Liberty and Justice for All call from the U.S. bishops because it included the role of women as one of its points of concentration. This call to action would indeed serve as a rallying point around which Chicago Catholic Women could organize its goals. We could overcome whatever negativity we experienced as women on the local level. Perhaps our main goal of changing this Church to include women on an equal basis would happen sooner than we had anticipated.

With this in mind, Chicago Catholic Women held its next meeting on April 10, 1975, at Trinity High School (1204 W. Jackson, River Forest), from 7 to 9 p.m. Women were encouraged to each bring another five to ten laywomen or sisters to this meeting. Women were called during this Holy Year to be reconcilers and, during the U.N. International Women's Year, to celebrate equality, development, and peace. Additionally, we were asked during the Bicentennial Celebration to set future policy for the Church in the United States.

So we set out to do just that. Over 125 women met that April 10 to discuss the problem areas that should receive attention, to begin the preparation of testimony, and to plan for a local hearing. We felt that it was important to give testimony in the Archdiocese of Chicago before taking our testimony to the regional hearing.

We planned for a hearing of testimony to be presented at Holy Name Cathedral in Chicago on June 1, 1975. We invited women to write and present their testimony. We sent a letter dated May 2, 1975, to several important people of the Church: the Cardinal, Auxiliary Bishops, Msgr. Brackin (the Archdiocesan Coordinator of the Bicentennial Program), the members of the Bicentennial Committee, the Directors of Diocesan Agencies, Officers of the Presbyteral Senate, the Presidents of the Archdiocesan Council of Catholic Women, the Association of Chicago Priests, the Leadership Conference of Women Religious (region VIII), the Conference of Major Superiors of Men, and the National Assembly of Women Religious. We invited them "to be a part of a panel to listen to and clarify the testimony and recommendations being made by women of the Catholic Church of Chicago. This testimony will also be part of the record for the Regional Bicentennial Conference to be held in St. Paul on June 12–14, 1975."[11] We knew we were the Church.

---

11 Sr. Donna Quinn, O.P., Chairperson of the June 1, 1975, hearing, and the Steering

Those who came and took their chairs on stage to listen to the testimony were four Archdiocesan Directors—from the Diocesan Clergy Personnel Board, the Archdiocesan Vocation Office, the Office of Divine Worship, and the Office for the Permanent Deaconate. Organizations represented by one or more persons were the Leadership Conference of Women Religious, Association of Chicago Priests, 8ᵗʰ Day Center for Justice, National Assembly of Women Religious, Presbyteral Senate of the Archdiocese, Conference of Major Superiors of Men, and the National Federation of Priests Councils. The chairperson of the day was Sister Albertus Magnus McGrath of Rosary College History Department.

One Auxiliary Bishop responded to our letter, indicating that he had another commitment. No response came from the Vicar of Religious, who was a priest. One of the 19 members of the Archdiocesan Bicentennial Committee attended; however, the coordinator did not respond. One woman who worked in an Archdiocesan office informed us after the April 10 meeting that she had to withdraw because she feared her job might be in jeopardy. This was one of the first indicators that we were going to have our work cut out for us.

On June 1, 1975, Chicago Catholic Women presented testimony from women for four and a half hours before a panel of 16 representatives of men and women of the Archdiocese and to an audience of over 200 people. We had empty chairs on the stage holding only a name card of the representatives who were invited and had not responded. The testimony we heard was

---

Committee of Chicago Catholic Women, Letter, 2 May 1975.

inclusive and wide-ranging: "The Contributions of Women to Ministry Today" by Lois McGovern, "The Oppression Which Black Women Experience Within the Church" by Margo Crawford, "Women in Prison" by Mary Powers, "Justice Education in the Church" by Peg Hanlon, "A Latino Women's Position in the Year of Women" by Dominga Zapata, "The Need for Ordained Women Priests and Deacons" by Patricia Hughes, "The Exclusion of Women from Decision-Making and Participation in the Church" by Terry Maltby, "Discriminatory Language in Ecclesiastical Documents and Liturgy" by Evangeline McSloy, "The Church and the Equal Rights Amendment" by Carolyn Parmer, and "Reconciliation—Male and Female" by Katherine Ward and Donna Marie Woodson.

Each testimony was heard, and the panel and observers responded. Some of the ensuing recommendations included:

- Appoint a woman religious as Associate Vicar for Religious; establish a committee of representatives of the various organizations of religious women for consultation on the appointment.
- Establish a committee of laywomen, women religious, laymen, and priests to monitor the status of women's participation at all levels in the Church and the Archdiocese; appoint a woman to chair this committee; again, consult with a committee or representatives of the various women's groups, both lay and religious, in the appointment of the members of this monitoring committee; and require the annual report of their findings to be

published in the diocesan newspaper.

- Provide in-service programs for bishops and clergy, and pre-service programs for seminarians on the developing role of women in Church and Society, to be conducted by women.

- Evaluate Chicago Archdiocesan women's organizations on the role they play in promoting an attitude of inferiority to male ecclesiastical administrators or contributing to a positive self-image in the members.

- Designate 50% of the seminary-support collection taken up in Chicago-area parishes as a scholarship fund for the theological education of women preparing for ordained ministry within the Archdiocese, and delete sexually discriminating references from this appeal and all other pulpit communications.

Another topic was presented that day...by the anti-choice movement. We were presenting testimony that was pro-ERA, and they wanted a small amount of time to present their opposing message. I learned a lesson from this that I would never forget. Back then I was all for giving everyone equal time and I trusted they would follow the parameters that were given to them, even if I didn't agree with their position on the matter. I am forever grateful that I had asked Sr. Albertus Magnus, O.P., to be the chairperson for the day.

Albertus Magnus, a history professor at Rosary College (now Dominican University), author of *What a Modern Catholic Believes about Women*—and a woman with a strong personality—

sat on the stage in the center of chairs for diocesan officials. In front of the panel were tables so they could take notes and comment on the testimony. A microphone was in the middle aisle. When the anti-choice person presented her testimony, she went over the time allotted. Albertus Magnus asked her to wrap it up. The presenter ignored her and kept going on and on, getting louder and louder. Albertus Magnus again told her to stop, but the presenter started shouting and her followers began clapping for her. Albertus Magnus finally took her shoe off and banged it repeatedly on the table in front of her. She was the first person I had ever seen take off her shoe to bring a meeting to order! There was dead silence. Sister Albertus Magnus stood up, stared at the audience, and called the meeting to an end. The woman and her followers stomped out. It was a scene one could never forget.

Teresa Maltby stated that "One of the most glaring injustices suffered by women employed by the Church in Chicago is the lack of opportunity to participate in leadership or decision-making roles of crucial diocesan agencies." Each agency, she noted, is headed by a priest, with only token input from female staff members. Further, she pointed out, there is no Sisters Senate to parallel the Priests Senate, the Sisters Advisory Council "was simply ignored out of existence by Cardinal Cody,"[12] and the Urban Apostolate of the Sisters will go out of existence this month because the Archdiocese had terminated its funding.[13] It was no wonder that the stage was set for a women's group to develop a plan to address the present discrimination experienced in the Church.

---

12 James Robinson, "Catholic Women Seek Voice in Archdiocese," *Chicago Tribune*, 2 June 1975.
13 Ibid.

—✤✤✤—

CCW's June 1 hearing was reported in the Chicago Arch-diocesan newspaper. On June 6, 1975, *The New World* printed an article "Strange Stories Appearing in Chicago Newspapers" and included the following:

> *The Chicago Tribune* seems to have fallen into the same trap as the field newspapers, with its story Monday about Chicago Catholic Women, and a front-page box proclaiming, "Catholic Women Challenge Cody on Church Bias." This is another odd one. The audience at that Sunday meeting of the group…according to news stories, seems to have proclaimed itself the spokeswomen for the Catholic women of the Archdiocese. They appear to have overlooked the Archdiocesan Council of Catholic Women, with about 250,000 members—very active in the affairs of the Church, in close contact with the officials of the Archdiocese, and definitely a voice for women. One has only to sit in on their meetings to know that…there is no feeling that they are being ignored by the Church in the Chicago Archdiocese. Perhaps the problem in this, as in other situations, is that some groups want not a voice, an opportunity to present views, but rather to make the decisions. And that is not their prerogative, their function. A great deal of bitterness and anger might be avoided if this were realized as one of the facts of life.[14]

---

14 "Strange Stories Appearing in Chicago Newspapers," *The New World*, 6 June 1975: 11.

On June 12, 1975, Marge Tuite and I flew up to St. Thomas College in St. Paul with testimony from our June 1 hearing in Chicago to be presented to the Liberty and Justice for All—A Call to Action regional hearing. On the plane, Marge and I looked over the paper that I would read to the assembly titled, "The Experience of Powerlessness in the Church." We were pleased with it. I felt excited, nervous, and responsible to the women of our newly formed organization—Chicago Catholic Women. We were listed in the program and finally on June 14, 1975, our time had come.

This is what I read:

> My name is Sister Donna Quinn. I am representing a group called Chicago Catholic Women—a growing grassroots movement of laywomen and women religious organized out of love for the Church and particularly the Church in Chicago. I talk today out of this experience.

We began last December with a concern for helping women in the Archdiocese of Chicago provide input to the bishops of the United States for the social justice policy formation. We responded to the bishops' call for grassroots participation in the Bicentennial Program. I would like to outline for you just what our experience has been in the Archdiocese of Chicago in this effort. We believe it rather vividly portrays the problems women face when we try to become involved in our Church. We hope that by hearing our testimony, you will better understand what women experience in our Church. This for us is an experience in powerlessness.

The Chicago Archdiocesan Bicentennial Committee is composed of nineteen members—only one of whom is a woman. We wrote to the chairman (chairperson), the Vicar General of the Archdiocese, requesting that at least one other woman, a woman religious, be added to the committee. For several weeks, we received no response. We finally called the chairman (chairperson) and we were told that a Jesuit priest on the committee was that representative for women religious. The chairman (chairperson) indicated that there was no need for women religious being on the central committee, since they could become involved on the parish level.

In February we requested information on the process for grassroots participation and were informed that a plan for local participation had not yet been formulated. It was then clear to us that since the St. Paul Regional Bicentennial Hearing was fast approaching, we would have to quickly develop a process if Chicago women were to have any input at all at this stage of the Bicentennial process. We contacted the Executive Director of the Bishops Committee for the Bicentennial to learn what procedures we should follow. We also sent two representatives to the Washington, D.C., Regional Hearing so that we might be better informed on the process.

We believe that the National Conference of Catholic Bishops must somehow come to terms with the problems of its own leadership in this area. Unnecessary obstacles continue to be placed in the way of women. We urge the bishops to involve themselves in a more intense exploration of the developing role of women.

We thank God for signs of hope such as the recent pastoral

letter of Bishop Dozier in "Women—Intrepid and Loving," and I close quoting his words: "Twentieth-century women cannot be expected to treasure those institutions which have limited her freedom, growth, and opportunity in life. In faith, she has remained faithful to the Church. But we must share the pained presence on those who seek to relate more maturely in love and service to the whole People of God. Let us hear, then, those voices that vocalize women's determination to assert her equality and profess her competence. Heedless institutions must inevitably pay the cost of indifference."[15]

After I read this statement, I remember walking to the back of the hall and standing with Marge Tuite, surrounded by a group of friends. The bishops assigned to listening to this testimony for the day assembled on the stage. Monsignor Brackin also took the stage representing Cardinal Cody. He went to the microphone and started screaming at me in anger. His face grew redder and redder as he yelled into the microphone that I did not represent an official group in the Chicago Archdiocese, that CCW was not part of the Diocesan Bicentennial Program, that we had no right to be here or to give testimony, and that our hearing at Holy Name Cathedral had not received Cardinal Cody's approval.

I only remember standing there in disbelief that someone in his position would be screaming at our input. His ranting only served to elevate Chicago Catholic Women as a courageous voice in the Church, focus on the discrimination of women in

---

15 Bishop Carroll T. Dozier, Pastoral Letter, "Women—Intrepid and Loving," (Memphis, 1975): 3.

the Church, and solidify our determination to work at the National Hearing in Detroit in October 1976.

CHAPTER 4
The National Meeting of the NCCB's Bicentennial Program

The New World reported that Cardinal Cody addressed the 45th Anniversary Luncheon of the Archdiocesan Council of Catholic Women on September 11, 1976, at the Conrad Hilton Hotel. "In a personal message to the Archdiocesan Council of Catholic Women, the Cardinal said, 'I always walk away from this gathering feeling on cloud 9. Whatever they may write or say about me, I know I have you women praying for me.' However, he pointed out that 'there is a group in this Archdiocese—who call themselves Chicago Catholic Women who would disrupt this unity.' He added that this organization has no affiliation with the Archdiocese and should not be confused with the ACCW."[16]

How many times did we see that in those early days of the movement? Always the strategy of playing women against women. I was careful to avoid going on TV or radio programs that might choose to do this to us—we were trying to build bridges, not be divisive.

Everything was new to us. We were making up the rules and setting policies as we went along. One thing we knew for sure was that the days of "nuns only" groups or "laywomen only" groups were over. Chicago Catholic Women was representative of both.

---

16   *The New World*, 17 September, 1976.

After the St. Paul Regional Bicentennial Hearing in June 1975, Chicago Catholic Women began having membership meetings on a monthly basis. We invited the Archdiocesan delegates to our September 30, 1976, membership meeting.

By then, the delegates to the Detroit Hearing selected by Msgr. Brackin were Cardinal Cody; Monsignor Brackin; Sisters Alexandria, Octavia Baker, Angele Cettini, Lorenz, Dorothy Lynch, and Margaret Niemeyer; Reverends Timothy Lyne, Wenceslaus Nadaj, Thomas Murphy, James Murtaugh, John O'Donnel, Raymond Pavis, James Roache, and Jerome Siwek; laypersons Peter Foote, Thomas Ewers, Miriam Helms, Joan Krebs, Carol Luczak, Veronica Rohr, Mary Jo Tulley, and Mrs. William Spencer. The delegation included 12 women and 12 men. This was a lot different than the all-male and one laywoman on the Bicentennial Committee, although again, we were given no part in the selection process.

A letter of invitation to our September 30 meeting went out to each delegate. On September 17, 1976, Monsignor Brackin wrote his own letter to each of the delegates:

> It appears that some confusion has arisen about a meeting being arranged by a group calling themselves Chicago Catholic Women. In the light of what follows this meeting will not be held.
>
> Chicago Catholic Women is not an authorized organization of the Archdiocese of Chicago and the meeting being called has nothing to do with the official Bicentennial Committee. The only official Archdiocesan group

of Catholic women (under the direction of the Reverend James Murtaugh) is the ARCHDIOCESAN COUNCIL OF CATHOLIC WOMEN.

The letter that was forwarded to you as a member of the official committee, was written without any ecclesiastical approval. The writer of the letter is not an officially appointed delegate for the Chicago Bicentennial Delegation. Regretting the annoyance that this has caused you, and with every good wish, I am,

Monsignor Francis A. Brackin[17]

Monsignor Brackin also sent a personal response to me and Chicago Catholic Women, saying he was very surprised to receive our invitation to the September 30 meeting, adding "...I do not see the need of meeting to hold special discussions on one aspect or in favor of one particular group at this time...Further, as a matter of Christian courtesy, I think the idea of inviting the Chicago delegation to your meeting should have been discussed with the Coordinator [Brackin referring to himself] before the notices were sent out."[18]

On September 29, 1976, I replied to Monsignor Brackin stating that we received his letter and were disappointed that he would not be able to attend the September 30 meeting but we would take minutes and would be happy to share a copy with him.

---

17 Msgr. Francis A. Brackin, Letter to Chicago Archdiocesan delegates for the Chicago Bicentennial Committee, 17 September, 1976.
18 Msgr. Francis A. Brackin, Letter to Chicago Catholic Women, 17 September 1976.

Chicago Catholic Women presented this exchange public-ly at our meeting of delegates on September 30, 1976, at Holy Name Cathedral. Prior to this meeting, one delegate sent us a letter saying that because she was employed by the Archdiocese, she feared for her job and would not attend the meeting. Peter Foote, Director of Archdiocesan Communications, was the only delegate who came to our meeting. Peter Foote, wanted to know just how many nuns and how many laity were in our group, and asked, "How many are laywomen?" All hands went up. "No, no," he said, "I mean, how many of you are sisters?" We looked at each other and smiled. I could have cried when every hand in the room went up. He had found frustration; we had found the true meaning of the Catholic feminist movement.

—⊗⊗⊗—

It was not a surprise to learn that Chicago Catholic Women was not granted official delegate status in Detroit for the Na-tional Hearing, October 21–23, 1976. I went as a delegate rep-resenting the National Coalition of American Nuns (NCAN). Other women in attendance from Chicago were Dolores Brooks, Rosalie Muschal Reinhardt, and Marge Tuite. We met up with some great women, including Ada Maria Isasi-Diaz, Joan Chittister, and Dolly Pomerleau. Another attendee was always there with us, Bishop Amadee Proulx from Portland, ME. He joined us everywhere—whether we were running across streets to find a place to eat with room for eight or ten, or just talking about our issues. We happily welcomed him in as a supportive member of our group. Our Chicago circle was always a part of a broader assembly of kindred spirits who were always talking, planning, and writing out recommendations that would later be accepted by the entire delegate body of 1,200. We stayed together as a group that became known as *the ones working out the women's recommendations*. One day while we were on the escalator, we heard some bishops talking to each other about the need to put a stop to "this group who had been the planners of the Women's Ordination Conference held the year before, and were now going too far with the issue of ordination."

By July 1976, according to the latest feedback of more than 800,000 respondents to the Liberty and Justice program's parish discussions, "the role of women in the Church was identified as a justice issue by more participants than any other single topic," according to Sister Alice Gallin, Director of Research for the program. This reflected a wide range of opinions: "The greatest number of respondents suggest that women should be free to do all ministries in the Church. Others urge that women should be ordained deacons, or should have an active role in decision-making at all levels in the Church, or should find fulfillment at home."[19]

The recommendations that we hammered out at the National Hearing came under the topic "Church," and were presented to the 1,340 delegates who acted as an advisory to the U.S. bishops. It was one of three resolutions: "Justice in the Church," "Women in the Church," and "Education." Under "Women in

---

19   U.S. Bishops, *U.S. Bishops Conference on Liberty and Justice for All: A Call to Action* Vol. 2, No. 6 (July 1966): 3.

the Church" we listed eight recommendations with the following preface:

> Vatican Council II has called the Church to a renewed sense of mission to the world, to its self-understanding of a people bearing responsibility for justice. The grave problems of the world challenge the Church to remove inherited structures which prevent full participation of its members in ministry and, thus to empower all of them for service according to their gifts and calls.
>
> Traditional Church life and practice have especially limited the freedom of women to share responsibility and ministry. The *Church in the Modern World*, no. 29, called for elimination of discrimination based on sex. Therefore, we recommend the following:
>
> 1. That the National Conference of Catholic Bishops in consultation with a body of representatives of each of the national Catholic organizations of women establish within the NCCB/USCC an effectively staffed structure to promote the full participation of women in the life and ministry of the Church and that this representative body design, develop, and implement such a staff structure.
>
> 2. That the National Conference of Catholic Bishops offer leadership in justice to the universal Church by providing a process which facilitates the formation of a more fully developed position on the ordination of women to sacred orders.

i. To be credible, this position must evolve from an open exploration of the rights and needs of persons and of the Christian community; the action of the Holy Spirit in the Church, and a collaborative and interpretive study of the human sciences, of the experiences of other Christian churches, of contemporary biblical exegesis of theological insights, as well as of pontifical and Episcopal statements. The study should involve appropriate organizations of scholars, lay and religious women, especially women who believe themselves called to the priesthood.

ii. A planned process and timeline sharing the interpretive study should be presented to the Catholic community by November 1977. [DQ: Little did we know then that by January 1977 an ominous Vatican statement, "Declaration on the Question of Women to Ministerial Priesthood," would be issued by Pope Paul VI.]

3. That an affirmative action plan be developed by the NCCB and local ordinaries, together with women representatives, to assure the equal status of women.

i. By effecting their participation in decision making and leadership at all levels of Church institutions, agencies, committees, and commissions.

ii. By guaranteeing women equal access to professional theological and pastoral training in seminaries, schools of theology, or other educational programs available for those involved in the work of the Church.

4. That the National Conference of Catholic Bishops and Catholic publishing houses act to insure that sexist language and imagery be eliminated from all official Church documents, catechisms, liturgical books, rites, and hymnals printed after January 1978.

5. That the Church identify, formally authenticate, and expand ministries being performed by women in the Church.

6. That women have equal opportunities for training as well as the authority and responsibility to perform the ministries effectively.

    i. To insure that all women have equal access to and full participation in roles of leadership, service, and authority in the life of the Church, we recommend that structures be developed on diocesan and parish levels.

    ii. These structures should be developed after consultation with representatives of local Catholic women's organizations and other interested women.

3. That Church law and prescriptions governing liturgical practices be reviewed and adapted to eliminate sexual discrimination.

4. That female children be granted the right and opportunity to serve at the altar in the role traditionally allowed to altar boys.

Our group worked with those focusing on "Personhood" in supporting the Equal Rights Amendment (the ERA was also endorsed under the section titled "Work"). The following was passed under the Second Resolution of Personhood, "Personal Development": "That social action agencies and offices give active support to efforts to achieve the legal rights and full economic justice for women in their local communities and in American society and to support efforts to inform women of their legal rights with the family, the work force, and the community in general. We endorse and support the Equal Rights Amendment of the Constitution."

The Third Resolution of Personhood was titled "Sexuality." Its fourth recommendation stated "that the Church actively seek to serve the pastoral needs of those persons with a homosexual orientation, to root out those structures and attitudes which discriminate against homosexuals as persons, and to join the struggle by homosexual men and women for their basic constitutional rights to employment, housing, and immigration. That the Church encourage and affirm the pastoral efforts of Dignity, the organization of gay and concerned Catholics, to reconcile the Church with its homosexual brothers and sisters."

It is important to note the topics of testimony and recommendations from our local hearing on June 1, 1975, and the recommendations that we worked out at the NCCB Bicentennial Hearing on October 23, 1976, in Detroit.

These became the backbone of Chicago Catholic Women's work for the next 25 years, and none but female altar servers have been resolved at the time of this writing.

CHAPTER 5

Continuing Our Work in the Seventies

Not everyone appreciated or identified with the recommendations that came out of the 1976 Detroit Conference. The president of the National Conference of Catholic Bishops, Archbishop Joseph L. Bernardin, said the meetings of 1,300 clergy, nuns, and laity from across the country acted, "without adequate reflection, discussion, and consideration of different points of view." The Conference, thought by many Catholics to be the most representative meeting of American Catholics in history, and the closest we had ever come to democracy in the Church, was said by Archbishop Bernardin to be "not representative of the Church in this country." He further stated, "Undoubtedly, many good recommendations emerged which will provide the groundwork for constructive reflection and action in the future, but to be realistic, others must be considered problematical at best."[20]

One big problem for Archbishop Bernardin was the emerging voice of women regarding ordination. In December 1974, a woman named Mary B. Lynch raised the question heard around the world, "Why not ordain women?" Mary, a student at Catholic Theological Union (CTU) and the first single laywoman in the country to receive a Masters of Divinity Degree,

---

20 James Robinson, "Archbishop Raps Reform Conference," *Chicago Tribune*, 27 October 1976.

thought it was time to entertain the question of women being ordained in the Catholic Church. She called a group together at CTU on December 13, 1974, to discuss the question. There were 28 women—all but two, Rosalie Muschal-Reinhardt and Mary B. Lynch, were nuns—and three men present.

One of those nuns was Joan O'Shea, a member of the religious community to which I belong. I remember her calling me while I was home on Christmas vacation and asking if I would take her place at the next meeting, which was to be held in March 1975. I was excited to be a part of this new, growing call for ordaining women. That was my first meeting on the matter, and I became dedicated to the cause for the years, which turned into the decades, that followed. These early days were exciting times and things were falling into place, or so I wanted to believe.

By June 1975, after organizing the Chicago Catholic Women Hearing and bringing this testimony to St. Paul, I knew I was being called to do this work rather than that of a classroom teacher. One way to discern whether or not to make such a transition in those days was to do a Clinical Pastoral Education (C.P.E.) program. Joan O'Shea had done the program and she encouraged Dolores Brooks and me to do one. We both applied and were accepted at Rush-Presbyterian St. Luke's Hospital on Chicago's West Side. That summer, we lived at nearby Holy Family and by August, I moved with a small group of Sinsinawa Dominicans to the North Side of Chicago. After our C.P.E. was completed, Dolores opted to study theology at Westin School of Theology in Cambridge, MA. I began working at paying jobs while trying to keep Chicago Catholic Women going.

—❀❀❀—

To be credible in the Archdiocese, Chicago Catholic Women needed a home with a mailing address and telephone number. During the summer of 1975, we were given a space at the 8th Day Center for Justice, located at 22 E. Van Buren St. We were grateful to 8th Day for granting us this space at their center as we had no money to pay for a director or rent. They were setting up a Justice Center and were always big-hearted to those in need. The staff persons there were Betty Barrett, Joanne Crowley, Chuck Dahm, Dorothy Gartland, Tom Joyce, and Beth Wagner.

Many people were generous with their talents to get Chicago Catholic Women started. Christian Molidor, R.S.M., and Gilmary Lemberg, S.S.N.D., for example, helped design the first stationery we used. I was the glue that held Chicago Catholic Women together. We never had money to pay for staff, and so in 1975 I taught Ministry of the Deaconate to women married to Archdiocesan deacons at Quigley Preparatory Seminary on the North Side.

—❀❀❀—

The second Chicago Catholic Women Coordinating Committee was set up and in place by 1976. Some women stayed on from the first 12-person coordinating committee. More women wanted to be on the second one and our number grew to 16. Members included Patricia Crowley; Barbara Davidson; Ella

Gardner; Teresina Grasso, S.P.; Georgia Mae Horrell; Patricia Hughes; Donna Moriarty Kennedy; Joan Krebs; Terry Maltby, R.S.M.; Lois McGovern, O.P.; Carolyn Noonan Parmer; Donna Quinn, O.P.; Maureen Reiff; Marilyn Steffel; Mary Sullivan, R.S.M.; and Marjorie Tuite, O.P. We definitely wanted more laywomen than nuns—or at least an equal number—because we believed that we are all sisters in the movement and wanted our new organization to reflect that.

These years meant meeting so many new people. There were the many people working on human rights issues who came to the 8th Day Center and those who were on staff there. Then there were the women of Chicago Catholic Women, interested in furthering the goals of our June 1975 hearing and eventually the final goals of the Detroit Bicentennial Conference of October 1976.

We held in admiration our sisters of the Episcopal Church, who were ordained to the priesthood on July 29, 1974. On that day, 11 women deacons from eight dioceses stepped forward: Merrill Bittner, Alla Bozarth-Campbell, Alison Cheek, Emily Hewitt, Carter Heyward, Suzanne Hiatt, Marie Moorefield, Jeannette Piccard, Betty Schiess, Katrina Swanson, and Nancy Wittig. Their ordinations were irregular, however, not because Canon Law prohibited women priests, but because they were not ordained by their own diocesan bishops, nor with the consent of the Standing Committees of the dioceses. The ordaining bishops, the Rt. Rev. Daniel Corrigan, the Rt. Rev. Robert DeWitt, and the Rt. Rev. Edward Welles, II, were not diocesan bishops with jurisdiction, but were instead either retired or resigned.

Alla Bozarth-Campbell wrote: "It is humbling to find oneself in a position of prophetic interplay with the authority of the Church. Each of us at times is called to challenge the body of which we are all a part, in this way claiming co-responsibility for the integrity of the whole. We all stand at different degrees of relationship to the whole, and each of us is called to respond from our unique angle of vision."[21]

We looked to the courage of women of other faith traditions so that we might learn from their struggle with the institutional male hierarchies. It was the right time for women from the Roman Catholic tradition to also stand up for what was right and just.

The women responding to the call of St. Joan's Alliance, NCAN, and now Mary B. Lynch for the ordination of women, did something very historical in March 1975. We decided that we would have our own national conference to discuss the ordination of women. This conference would take place in Detroit, MI, on Thanksgiving weekend, November 28–30, 1975, and would be called "Women in Future Priesthood Now: A Call for Action."

The taskforce members for this first conference were 21 in all, 17 nuns and four laywomen: Rosemary Bearss, R.S.C.J.; Dolores Brooks, O.P.; Monica Brown, O.P.; Joan Campbell, S.L.; Avis Clendenen, R.S.M.; Anne Mary Dooley, S.S.J.; Mary Ann Flanagan, I.H.M.; Nadine Foley, O.P.; Louise Hageman, O.P.; Patricia Hughes; Ann Kelley, S.N.D.; Mary B. Lynch; Donna Quinn, O.P.; Rosalie Muschal-Reinhardt; Mary Schaefer;

---

21 Alla Bozarth-Campbell, *Womanpirest: A Persona. Odyssey,* (New York: Paulist Press, 1978): 121.

Mary Ellen Sheehan, I.H.M.; Marilyn Sieg, S.F.C.C.; Karen Stepien, I.H.M.; Margaret Urban, O.P.; Georgene Wilson, O.S.F.; and Michaela Zahner, C.S.J.

Word of our event spread quickly. We had no idea that so many women and men from across the U.S.A., Belgium, Canada, and Australia would come to such a conference. We planned for 600 and when the numbers reached 1,200 we moved the function to the Sheraton-Southfield Hotel in Detroit. The Conference Taskforce of 21 women hoped to "raise the concern about ordained ministry for women as an issue with national visibility."

We did this around three goals:

1. To convene persons committed to making the talents of women fully available for ministerial service in the Roman Catholic Church;

2. To inform the people of God about women preparing for a new expression of full priesthood; and

3. To provide a forum in which participants could examine the present status of the ordination issue and develop strategies for effective action.[22]

This was the first conference of its kind, and for us it was the process, and not only the input, that was very important. Marge Tuite, O.P., served as strategist; Mary Daniel Turner,

---

22 Anne Marie Gardiner, S.S.N.D., Editor, *Women and Catholic Priesthood: An Expanded Vision—Proceedings of the Detroit Ordination Conference* (New York: Paulist Press, 1976), "A Process Model for Theological Reflections and Actions," by Nancy Lafferty, F.S.P.A., 165.

S.S.N.D. was synthesizer; Nancy Lafferty, F.S.P.A., was process consultant; and Judith Vaughan, C.S.J., compiled and tab-
ulated a questionnaire profiling participants and their wish to
be ordained. A process model would implement the three goals
of the conference, and have as its major objective "to create a
climate in which both theological and scriptural reflection and
just actions could take place. It became evident that participants were interested in having theological and scriptural issues
explicated by scholars, share their experiences of their own diverse ministries, and express hopes and plans for the future."[23]

---

23 Ibid., 166.

CHAPTER 6

The Founding of Women's Ordination Conference: The Vatican Takes Notice

The next National Women's Ordination Conference we organized would not be until October 1978; but between 1975 and 1978 efforts were made by the Vatican and bishops in the U.S. to try to quell the fire lit by that call to ordain women.

On October 3, 1975—how poignant to issue this on the feast day of St. Therese of Lisieux—the Archbishop of Cincinnati and President of the National Conference of Catholic Bishops (NCCB), Joseph Bernardin, was authorized to make a statement reaffirming the Church's teaching that women were not to be ordained to the priesthood. The Bishops' Committee on Pastoral Research and Practice had issued a report in 1972 entitled *Theological Reflections on the Ordination of Women*. Archbishop Bernardin used this often in his statement to the media. He referred to a longstanding tradition, which was not referring simply to a custom but to a teaching of the Ordinary Magisterium and this, though not formally defined, was for him Catholic doctrine. He went on to call it a mistake to reduce the question of the ordination of women to one of injustice, as is done at times.[24]

---

24 Anne Marie Gardiner, S.S.N.D., Editor, *Women and Catholic Priesthood: An Expanded Vision—Proceedings of the Detroit Ordination Conference* (New York: Paulist Press, 1976), "The Bernardin Statement—U.S.C.C. News Statement," 3 October 1975: 193–198.

As the weekend of our National Conference approached, Bernardin came out with another statement, issued on November 20, 1975:

"The reason for this statement is because by now the issue of the ordination of women has become a topic of lively discussion within the Church. The Bishops of the Administrative Committee, who authorized me to make the statement, felt that in the light of the discussion taking place their position should be made clear."

Bernardin went on to say the "precise question is: Was the exclusion of women from the priesthood by Christ determined simply by the cultural situation which existed in His day. Or did Christ exclude women for other reasons...Was it His will, in other words, that only men be called to the ordained ministry as a matter of principle?"

"The Church has taught that it was Christ's will that only men be called to the priesthood. When the Bishops' Committee on Pastoral Research and Practice in 1972 referred to a longstanding tradition, they were not referring simply to a custom but to a teaching that has been constant; one that has been questioned only in recent years. It is because the bishops do not see any development on the horizon which is of sufficient weight to overturn this teaching that they felt obligated to reaffirm it."

Bernardin continued: "any study of this question should take place within the following framework:

1. It must be done in accord with the accepted norms
    of theological research.

2. It must take into account the fact that the Church's constant tradition has been not to ordain women and that this fact does have significance in Catholic theology.

3. There must be a willingness ultimately to accept the judgment of the Magisterium. Any study which is not carried on within this framework will, in my judgment, be of little value.[25]

Meanwhile women were not to be deterred from their goal of working for the ordination of women. At the end of the Women's Ordination Conference held in Detroit in 1975, the assembly of 1,400 participants (one-tenth from the Chicago area) approved a proposal that asked for the formation of a national organization around the issue of the ordination of women in the Catholic Church.

In March 1976, 45 participants met at Catholic Theological Union in Chicago and adopted the name Women's Ordination Conference for the organization. The main goal of WOC would be the ordination of women in a renewed priestly ministry.

An ad hoc committee designed a selection process for a core commission to lead this newly formed organization. With nationwide participation, 183 names surfaced. Of these, 22 women were selected to serve on the first core commission for two years.

Nineteen women were able to accept:

25 Ibid., "News Conference—Archbishop Bernardin's Statement," 20 November 1975: 197–198.

Mary Beckman

Dolores Brooks, O.P.

Rose Colley, S.L.

Nadine Foley, O.P.

Ann Hallisey

Donna Quinn, O.P.

Sonya Quitslund

Kathleen Marie Henderson

Glenna Raybell, O.S.B.

Dolly Pomerleau

Shawn Scanlan, S.S.N.D.

Sue Secker, O.P.

Marge Tuite, O.P.

Ada Maria Isasi-Diaz

Sylvia Sedillo, S.L.

Judi Kepperlich

Rosalie Muschal-Reinhardt

Rosemary Kutz

Mary Beth Onk

From June 25 to June 27, 1976, the first core commission of WOC held their first meeting at Rosary College (now Dominican University) in the near Chicago suburb of River Forest. There, Mary B. Lynch was named member *emeritus pro vitae* on the core commission. A decision was made to ask for delegate status at the NCCB's Bicentennial Call to Action Conference to be held in October of that year.

By September 1976, delegate status was denied to WOC but WOC challenged the Credential Committee of the Call to Action Bicentennial Conference and attained authorization for Rosalie Muschal-Reinhardt to attend as our official delegate.

The WOC Core Commission made three important moves in 1977:

1. They asked Ruth Fitzpatrick to serve as a full-time office director for WOC in Washington, D.C.
2. They supported Episcopal women at the Episcopal

Convention, which voted to ordain women in the Episcopal Church in the U.S.

3. They voted to have another conference in 1978

News of another conference was greeted by most women with joy and anticipation. There was never a thought that we couldn't do it. We would build on the 1975 WOC Conference and decided to move it out east to Baltimore.

Whenever women sensed a little success regarding gender advancements, another statement was proclaimed by the Church hierarchy to attempt to silence the masses. This time it was not something from Bernardin but—at the urging of the bishops—a statement from Pope Paul VI.

This statement was written in December 1976—after the 1975 WOC Conference and the NCCB Bicentennial Conference in October 1976. The statement was issued in January 1977 and titled, "The Declaration on the Question of the Admission of Women to Ministerial Priesthood." Now the Vatican had gone too far. The statement was ludicrous, not only to Catholics, but to those who were not Catholic. People were appalled and dismayed that such a statement could actually be taken seriously. It was embarrassing to belong to the Catholic tradition. It said that women cannot participate in the priesthood because they do not resemble the maleness of Christ. For us, it called into question our Baptism, the Mystical Body of Christ, the concept of the risen Jesus, now called Christ, and the continued policy of discrimination by the Vatican against women.

I remember those days and evenings of gatherings about

this declaration. One such meeting took place in our living room on the North Side of Chicago with Marge Tuite, Carroll Stuhlmueller, Anne Carr, Dolores Brooks, Rosemary Radford Ruether, Sue Secker, Rosalie Muschal-Reinhardt, and myself. I sat in amazement at these great minds. I remember listening in wonder at how rapidly Rosemary could absorb, synthesize, and communicate her thoughts for a statement that we would publish for Chicago Catholic Women locally and for WOC nationally. If only the Pope had surrounded himself with such brilliant people. What a different statement he could have made—one that would have made us proud to know him. Another missed opportunity by the Vatican.

We knew at this point that we needed a coalition of organizations with similar agendas to work together not only for ordination but for other gender issues. Dolores Brooks, Rosalie Muschal-Reinhardt, and I decided to call for such a meeting of organizations across the country.

From May 3 to May 4, 1977, the National Conference of Catholic Bishops met at the Palmer House in Chicago. At that time, the NCCB met twice a year—in Chicago in May and in Washington, D.C., in November. One item on their agenda in Chicago, May 1977, was the recommendations on women from the NCCB's Bicentennial Call to Action Conference (Detroit 1976). Rosalie Muschal-Reinhardt, Dolores Brooks, and I from Chicago Catholic Women invited some other groups to join with Chicago Catholic Women at the Palmer House: Leadership Conference of Women Religious (LCWR), National

Coalition of American Nuns (NCAN), National Assembly of Women Religious (NAWR), Women's Ordination Conference (WOC), St. Joan's Alliance, Institute of Women Today, Christian Feminists, Las Hermanas, National Black Sisters Conference, National Sisters Vocation Conference, and Priests for Equality. We rented a room at the Palmer House, posted a WOMEN OF THE CHURCH COALITION sign outside the room and leafleted the bishops, asking them to join us in dialogue about justice issues for women.

There was an existing coalition called Sisters Uniting, which had only nuns' groups in its membership, sharing work on women's issues. There was tension over having two coalitions with some of the same organizations belonging to both. But our two organizations Chicago Catholic Women (est. 1974) and Women's Ordination Conference (est. 1975) had the power of both nuns and women who were not nuns. I remember sitting in a coffee shop next to the Palmer House prior to the NCCB meeting with Marge Tuite and members of LCWR. LCWR wanted to meet with Marge and me regarding this new coalition. Their concern was mainly with the composition of WOC and the ordination issue. Did we think this new group with laywomen was valid and credible? LCWR considered withdrawing from our coalition but Marge and I asked them to reconsider, however clearly said that despite how much we needed LCWR to stay in the coalition, we were not willing to ask WOC to leave the group. WOC was in to stay and that was how we left it. LCWR decided to stay in our Women of the Church Coalition.

—❀❀❀—

- Sonya Quitslund, Christian Feminists
- Rosalie Muschal-Reinhardt, Women's Ordination Conference
- Kathleen Keating, National Assembly of Women Religious
- Ruth Fitzpatrick, Women's Ordination Conference
- Betty Barrett, Leadership Conference of Women Religious
- Donna Quinn, National Coalition of American Nuns and Chicago Catholic Women

These women met with the NCCB committee on the Role of Women in Society and the Church in August 1977 in Washington, D.C. When the first point of our women's agenda from the National Call to Action Conference—"that the National Conference of Catholic Bishops in consultation with a body of representatives of each of the national Catholic organizations of women establish within the NCCB/USCC an effectively staffed structure to promote the full participation of women in the life and ministry of the church and that this representative body design, develop, and implement such a staff structure,"— changed to focus on getting membership on the NCCB committee, we worked with this committee but to no avail. We did not want representation as individuals but rather as representatives from the Women of the Church Coalition. We were viewed as too strong and they did not want to deal with the issue of ordination.

By September 1978, a new core commission of the Women's Ordination Conference (WOC) was selected after consultation with the constituency. I introduced them to the assembly at the Women's Ordination Conference held November 10–12, 1978, in Baltimore. Ruth Fitzpatrick completed her years as coordinator of Women's Ordination Conference, allowing Rosalie Muschal-Reinhardt and Ada Maria Isasi-Diaz to become the new coordinators of WOC and move the office from Washington, D.C., to Rochester, NY. A year later, in September 1979, Joan Sobala joined Rosalie and Ada and they began dialogue meetings with the bishops. In the fall of 1980, a third core commission was selected, skills workshops and retreats were held around the country, and dialogue with the bishops continued.

— ❀❀❀ —

It was on December 8, 1979, that Chicago Catholic Women and Illinois Women's Ordination Conference protested the ordination of six Jesuits (five as deacons and one as a priest). This was held in Hyde Park at St. Thomas the Apostle Church. We stood in silent protest, wearing blue armbands. It would be the first of many protests at ordinations.

The newly formed Women of the Church Coalition designated April 30, 1980, "Women of the Church Day," to celebrate St. Catherine of Siena and women everywhere; we urged the wearing of blue arm bands and standing in churches or cathedrals to protest the men-only ordination policy.

We went out to Saint Mary of the Lake Seminary Chapel in Mundelein, IL, to protest ordinations of diocesan men there. When they changed the location to Holy Name Cathedral, we were there, always leafleting so that passersby and participants would know what we were doing. Many nodded their heads in agreement with our cause; some families were very angry that we were "spoiling this family event." I don't think they understood that this was bigger than one individual who called himself to ordination. Some of the families of those to be ordained, however, did talk with us about how women would one day be ordained too.

Every year the security at the ordinations got tighter. Invitations were needed to be allowed inside the Cathedral. Seats were at a premium. I don't know how we got away with it but in May 1981, while our group was gathered outside singing, Barbara Ferraro and I snuck in while the usher/guard had his head turned the other way. We quickly sat in the back pew. After we got in, I turned to Barbara and said, "What am I going to do? I cannot say the words as I do not want to be ordained." Barb looked at me and said, "Just say them for the women who could not get inside." At that moment the door to the Cathedral swung open and we could hear our protestors singing with joy that two of us made it inside. When Cardinal Cody asked those to be ordained "Are you ready and willing?" Barbara and I each shouted from the back pew, "Yes, I am ready and willing!"

With that, an older woman in the pew ahead of us pulled

her scarf off her neck and wrapped it very tightly around Barb's wrists. She kept making it tighter and tighter. I tried to stop her while calling for an usher. When the usher came over, saw that the woman almost cut into Barb's wrists and they were turning red, he pulled the scarf off and told the woman to turn around or she would be thrown out. Soon after, Cardinal Cody announced that someone had shot Pope John Paul II in Vatican Square. I will never forget the looks on faces. It felt like everyone had turned around to stare at Barb and me, as if we had brought about his demise, but clearly we were all in shock.

CHAPTER 7
Funding Women in Theological Studies and
Finding Work for Women in the Church

The Annual Seminary Collection (for male seminarians only) was scheduled to be taken up in all Chicago parishes on February 6, 1977. In response, Chicago Catholic Women began a Women's Pastoral Education Fund, an alternative to the Archdiocesan Seminary Collection. CCW Coordinating Committee got the word out by publishing the following notice in the *Chicago Sun-Times* and the *Chicago Daily News:*

> Women and men are called to serve the needs of God's people. There are Roman Catholic Seminaries and Schools of Theology, some in Chicago, currently preparing women to assume positions of shared responsibility and decision-making in the Church.
>
> On February 5th and 6th, Roman Catholic parishes in the Chicago Archdiocese will take up a collection to educate men for leadership in the Church. As an alternative for those who desire to experience JUSTICE in the Church, Chicago Catholic Women establishes the Women's Pastoral Education Fund. Send your contribution to: Women's Pastoral Education Fund

22 East Van Buren Street, Chicago, Illinois 60605

Witness to JUSTICE by placing this message in the Seminary Collection at your parish this coming weekend.[26]

The fund was aimed at narrowing the gap between that which is and that which ought to be, "thereby contributing to our growth as a more humane, just, and loving Church."[27] For two years CCW encouraged its members to place fake money, or "funny money" as we called it, in the Annual Seminary Collection and instead send real money to a women's organization of their choice. The money collected for our two grants was designed to contribute to the change of those systems and structures in the Catholic Church, which deny to women full participation in ministry and in decision-making and that diminish women's sense of self-worth as members of the Church.

For the 1977–78 school year there were 21 women full-time M.Div. candidates and 32 women studying theology on a part-time basis at the Jesuit School of Theology–Chicago. At Catholic Theological Union there were two women studying full-time for their Master of Divinity degrees and 22 women working on other theological degrees.[28]

In September 1978, CCW was able to present two women of the Chicago area with scholarship checks for the 1978–79 school year. Anne Metzler won a $400 grant to be put toward her M.A. in the Institute of Creation-Centered Spirituality, a one-year program out of the Theology Department at Munde-

---

26 Chicago Catholic Women, *UPDATE*, February 1977.
27 Chicago Catholic Women, *UPDATE*, October 1978.
28 Chicago Catholic Women, *UPDATE*, November 1977.

lein College; and Madalynn Smith would use her grant of $300 toward a Masters of Divinity Degree at the Jesuit School of Theology–Chicago.

We were very proud of our ability to help women continue their theological studies. However, we did not go unnoticed by the opposition. The taunting from some continued—for example, the pastor of St. Christopher's parish mailed a copy of the parish bulletin, with the following written across: "Dear Sister: Many thanks for giving the collection more publicity!—Fr. Brown." The arrow pointed to the results of his parish's Archdiocesan Seminary Collection: The collection amounted to $1,642.09; the previous year's total was $897.80. We were not deterred.

In addition to theological education opportunities, we were also interested in helping members learn about systemic sexism in Church and society. Chicago Catholic Women's newsletter, *UPDATE,* included an announcement of a conference co-sponsored by Chicago Catholic Women and the Leadership Conference of Women Religious on April 2, 1977, at Alvernia High School called "Women: Touching Common Ground." Anne Wilson Schaef led the discussion.

CCW worked on behalf of those looking for employment. Our *UPDATE* newsletters asked: *If you know of openings, either part time or full time, let us know.* This effort to find employment for members took another turn. In a letter dated January 18, 1978, on Chicago Catholic Women stationery, I wrote:

Dear Father,

Chicago Catholic Women is an organization whose purpose is to call women of the Archdiocese of Chicago to full participation in the mission of the Church. We have tried to offer to women employment in parishes involving many ministries to the people of that parish.

We ask your assistance now in our Employment Program for 1978. Would you please send to us the form at the bottom of this page?

Thank you for all that you do to bring the message of Jesus to the people of Chicago.

Blessings on your work in the New Year.

Sincerely,

Donna Quinn, O.P.,

for Chicago Catholic Women[29]

The form at the end of the page asked for two things: a brief description of the needs of the parish regarding ministry positions for women, and a contact person with name and telephone number. This letter was sent to every pastor in the Archdiocese—approximately 450. Three days after delivery, we received a letter from the Office of the Archbishop of the Archdiocese, addressed to every pastor in the Archdiocese of Chicago. It read:

To the Reverend Pastors and Administrators of the Arch-

---

29 Donna Quinn, O.P., for Chicago Catholic Women, Letter to Chicago Archdiocese pastors, 18 January 1978.

diocese:

> It has been brought to the attention of the Cardinal that a [take note of the "a"] Sister Donna Quinn, O.P., whose mailing address is given as 22 East Van Buren Street, Chicago, Illinois, has sent an offer to the parishes to find employment for women "in parishes involving many ministries to the people of that parish."
>
> This organization which calls itself "Chicago Catholic Women" has no authorization from the Archdiocese and has no approval to function as an employment agency. The Reverend Pastors and Clergy are respectfully advised that the Archdiocese does not approve of such a program.
>
> In addition, may we remind you that this same group is attempting to sabotage the Seminary Collection scheduled for February 4–5.
>
> Further, this group has no connection whatsoever with the Archdiocesan Council of Catholic Women.
>
> THE CHANCERY OFFICE
>
> P.S. You are asked to share the contents of this letter with your Associates.[30]

Roy Larson, Religion Editor of the *Chicago Sun-Times*, wrote an article in response to the Chancery's letter focusing on the dismissiveness of the "a" in "a Donna Quinn." Dated February 18, 1978, the article, "Nun Rates an 'A' – and It's Not Meant as A Compliment," stated, "What a difference an 'a' makes. If

---

30 Chancery Office, Letter to Reverend Pastors and Administrators of the Archdiocese, 23 January 1978.

it were any smaller it wouldn't be a word at all. Is it a Pastoral or a Juridical letter from the Chancery? Sometimes the Church resembles 'the household of faith, the family of God' that it is called to be. Sometimes it looks and sounds like just one more vast and cold bureaucracy. What a difference an 'a' makes!"[31]

Soon after this January letter from the Chancery, Chicago Catholic Women began to notice and feel heightened repercussions. We had a difficult time finding a parish to hold our events. We sent a letter to all pastors asking to use a hall in their parish to hold a fundraiser. Not many responded, but Holy Trinity did say "Yes." So, we planned, invited, and announced our First Annual Fundraiser for Saturday, March 4, 1978, from 8 to 11 p.m. at Holy Trinity Parish Hall, 1900 W. Taylor St. We were to have door prizes, raffles, music, refreshments, and available child care. We were going to award scholarships to women applying to the Women's Ministerial Fund.

Three days before the event, we were informed by the pastor that we could not have our fundraiser at Holy Trinity. We learned that in light of the Chancery's letter, we were no longer welcome. I called and asked the pastor to reconsider, but he would not. In the end we sent a letter itemizing the cost of printing and advertising, and he sent us a check for $120 to cover the costs.

Six months later, Chicago Catholic Women was making the final arrangements for the use of a room at Holy Name Cathedral for our scheduled December 3 meeting. At this meeting we planned to reflect on the experience of the women and men

---

31 Roy Larson, "Nun Rates an 'A'—And It's Not Meant as a Compliment," *Chicago Sun-Times*, 18 February 1978: 24.

who would be attending the Baltimore Ordination Conference (November 10–12, 1978). Announcements were sent to the members of CCW, to the 140 attendees of the Baltimore Conference from the Chicago area, and to the 442 parishes in the Archdiocese.

One response from Monsignor Hagarty should have been a taste of what would follow. His response to our November 15, 1978, letter to the parish asking to place a notice in their bulletin regarding the December 3 CCW meeting was written in black felt pen across the letter: *Dear Donna— Save the postage. Your announcement has as much chance of getting into our bulletin as the proverbial "snowball" —Msgr. Hagarty, St. Norbert's.*

On November 26, 1978, one week prior to our meeting, Rev. Timothy Lyne, Pastor of Holy Name, contacted CCW and said that Cardinal Cody had called him to say CCW could not meet there because the American bishops did not attend the Women's Ordination Conference in Baltimore, (though Bishop Buswell from Pueblo, Colorado, was at the conference), and because of the Pope's position on the ordination of women, it would be inappropriate and personally embarrassing to the Cardinal for the meeting to take place at the Cathedral.

This time we refused to be cancelled and we searched around the neighborhood of Holy Name Cathedral for another church to take us in. We knew that we were not welcome at Catholic facilities, so we called the priest at St. Chrysostom's Episcopal Church. He was so wonderful to us, in stark contrast to our own. I will always remember him saying, "If you cannot discuss ordination in a Church, where else can you discuss this issue?

Of course you are welcome to use the Episcopal Church on December 3." I felt a rush of gratitude toward him and the people of that church. It was as if for the first time I knew what sacrament was and what reconciliation meant; I knew what their spirit of hospitality would mean to our members.

It was a bitterly cold, still December night when approximately 100 women and men gathered on the steps of Holy Name. We announced that Chicago Catholic Women was not welcome inside and then we walked the eight blocks to St. Chrysostom Episcopal Church at 1400 N. Dearborn Pkwy., where we were warmly welcomed for dialogue. No longer would women be silenced. No longer would our efforts to enter into dialogue be stopped. We are Church—the Roman Catholic Church. Our efforts will not cease until we have a Church which supports human rights—equal rights of every member. Thanks to those women and men who had the courage, vision, and belief to stand with, walk with, and dialogue with our members on December 3.[32]

What happened that night to Chicago Catholic Women represented where the hierarchy was regarding women. Cardinal Cody's message that night was clear. The Vatican's message in 1977 was clear. We were thought of as outsiders. This was their Church. This was their Jesus—all male. This night stood in stark contrast to the relationships we experienced at the Baltimore Ordination Conference a month prior to this gathering.

—❀❀❀—

---

32 Chicago Catholic Women, *UPDATE*, December 1978.

In our October 1978 newsletter, Chicago Catholic Women published its comparative study of women in Archdiocesan offices, using numbers from 1975 when CCW formed, and current 1978 figures. The Vicar for Religious was a man for 7,000 nuns and 3,000 priests in 1975, and 6,000 nuns and 2,500 priests in 1978. The Catholic Charities Board was totally male in 1975 and totally male in 1978. There were 885 lay employees (nuns were not counted). The school board remained the same—four out of 14 were women in both years. In 1975 the Superintendent of Schools was a male. In 1978 the new Vicar for Catholic schools was a male. In 1975 the Office of Arbitration and Conciliation had two women and seven men. In 1978 the office was inoperative. In the CCD office, five divisions were headed by men; seven men formed its Executive Committee with one woman assistant to the director. In 1978 the CCD office had five divisions headed by men; four men plus one woman formed the Executive Committee. In 1975 five of nine members on the Liturgical Board were women. In the Campaign for Human Development, five of 36 members were women; in 1978, 16 of 40 members were women. There were no women in the 1975 Marriage Tribunal; by 1978, still no women and 14 men acted as judges. In the Archdiocesan Directory, zero women were listed in both 1975 and 1978.[33]

—❀❀❀—

CCW also conducted a study of women in ministry in the

---

33   Chicago Catholic Women, *UPDATE*, October 1978.

Archdiocese and reported the findings in the November 1978 newsletter. Of the 261 city parishes, there were 39 nuns and four laywomen in pastoral ministry. In the 181 suburban parishes, there were 21 nuns hired as pastoral ministers. The city parishes hired 31 nuns and 17 laywomen as religious education coordinators while the suburban parishes employed 73 nuns and 56 laywomen as religious education coordinators.[34]

In order to do this study, pastors and associate pastors were contacted for the information. The priests for the most part were cooperative though some were hesitant to give information out to an "unauthorized" group. The following conclusions were reached after talking with the parishes:

1. A professional understanding of women as an integral part of parish staff is lacking.

2. The role of women is regarded as that of "helping priests."

3. There is a tendency to think of ministry as part-time work done mostly by "the nuns" in their "spare" time.

4. The idea of a woman as associate pastor is alien to most thought patterns.

5. If priests are available, there seems to be no reason or need to hire a woman.

6. There is often the tendency to find someone to do the work without having to hire that person.

This study ended with several questions: Will the parishes in

---

34   Chicago Catholic Women, *UPDATE*, November 1978.

Chicago be ready to hire a woman as an associate pastor? Why is it that women are not "ordained" to this call to minister? Why is it that women cannot preach on a regular basis in our Church? How much longer will women be willing to ask these questions in the institutional Church that we know today?[35]

—❀❀❀—

A letter dated January 11, 1978, was written to Cardinal Cody by Chicago Catholic Women stating that, "We note with sadness the resignation of Father Bob Clark from the Diocesan School Office…. It is our concern now that the process for the selection of a new superintendent be both open and professional…. We strongly urge that a search committee be constituted which represents the experiences of those involved in the Catholic school system in Chicago—parents and professional educators, lay and religious, women and men, reflecting the sexual, racial, and ethnic composition of the system itself…. It is our understanding that his Eminence will be sensitive to the Church as an Equal Opportunity Employer and so will seriously consider for the appointment persons of different sex and race."[36]

Cardinal Cody's response was quoted in *The Chicago Catholic*, January 27, 1978. "The selection of a new superintendent of Catholic schools, 'will be handled by the Board of Consultors and John Cardinal Cody'…The explanation came after, what the spokesman described as an 'unrecognized group' publicly

---

35 Ibid.
36 Chicago Catholic Women, Letter to Cardinal Cody, 11 January 1978.

calling for creation of a special search committee."[37]

Chicago Catholic Women's April 1978 *UPDATE* listed the consultors on this board: Most Rev. Alfred Abramowicz, Rev. Edward Detloff, Most Rev. Nevin Hayes, Rev. John Keating, Rev. Msgr. Francis Brackin, Rev. Arthur Krueger, Rev. Msgr. Thomas Holbrook, Rev. Timothy Lyne, Rev. Msgr. Robert Hagarty, Rev. Leonard Mattei, Rev. Msgr. Richard Rosemeyer, Rev. James Moriarty, Very Rev. Thomas Murphy, Rev. James Murtaugh, and Rev. Raymond Pavis.

UPDATE reported, "The consultors and the Cardinal met to make decisions about the Archdiocese of Chicago School System, which is the largest Catholic school system in the U.S. and the fourth largest school system in this country after Chicago Public Schools, N.Y. and L.A. Public Schools. Their answer is the newly-created position of Archdiocesan Vicar for Catholic Education *(Chicago Catholic,* March 24, 1978). No longer do we have a Superintendent of Schools. We have another Vicar in our Archdiocese—another cleric in a leadership role."[38]

Chicago Catholic Women's April 1978 issue of *UPDATE* published an article I wrote that stated, "The consultative process of this appointment is truly a return to pre-Vatican days. Was there not one among that great board of 15 Diocesan consultors who would take a stand on the fact that the people of our Archdiocese share in this decision and that CCW's position of a Search Committee and Selection process would have included both women and men? How many women are consultors

---

37   *The Chicago Catholic*, 27 January 1978.
38   Chicago Catholic Women, *UPDATE*, April 1978.

in this diocese? Is education not the one field where so many women have drained their last ounce of blood? Have we not been the mothers who have given birth to the children of this diocese? Have we as nuns not been the women who creatively taught in and changed the whole educational system and, I might add, used religious community resources to educate our women to that purpose? It is certainly not for want of credentials that women are excluded from diocesan decision-making. I, for one, am tired of hearing what 'a nice guy' the Vicar of Education is. If he were selected after a shared process by women and men of this Archdiocese, we might have cause to celebrate. It is one more example of a cleric—hand-picked by other clerics and the Cardinal—in this male-dominated decision-making process we experience in Chicago."[39]

—❀❀❀—

By March 18–20, 1979, a gathering of over 300 social action leaders from all over the U.S. was called to meet in Washington, D.C., to look again at the implementation of recommendations from the 1976 Bicentennial National Conference in Detroit. The role of women in the Church was not on the agenda of the three-day meeting which was planned as a "skills workshop" to assist parish leaders in effecting justice in both the Church and society.

Two specified incidents forced the issue onto the agenda. The first occurred before the meeting began when two women from

---

39 Ibid.

the Women's Ordination Conference (Rosalie Muschal-Reinhardt and Ada Maria Isasi-Diaz) sought unsuccessfully to register for the sessions. Frank Butler, who directed the Bicentennial National Call to Action Conference for the NCCB said
the meeting, was "not intended to be an issue conference."[40]

We leafleted in the hotel hallways. Merle Nolde, Karen
Minnice, and I were there for Chicago Catholic Women. Finally, Archbishop John Roach of St. Paul-Minneapolis, Chairperson of the Bicentennial National Call to Action Committee
of the NCCB, reversed his earlier decision and allowed us to
attend as observers. There must have been at least 15 of us there.
We could not believe that the NCCB had erased all of our work
from Detroit, citing in particular that ordination was out of the
question and the Vatican had responded to this.

The next thing that happened was that Msgr. John Egan,
one of the leaders at the Bicentennial National Call to Action
Conference, was to lead us in celebrating the Liturgy. He had
asked a friend, Sandra Galazin, a nun fighting for the rights of
lepers in Honolulu, to be the homilist. After asking Sandra,
Egan remembered that he would have to get permission for
this from the bishop of Washington, D.C. The bishop did not
give permission, so Egan had to take back his offer of a woman
doing the homily. This angered the women who were present.
We decided to stand at the time of Egan's homily and march
out of the room. Egan was stunned and, in his closing remarks
summarizing the conference, likened "the women's issue in the

---

40 Marjorie Hyer, *The Washington Post*, 23 March 1979.

Church today to the problems of racism in the sixties. The sin of injustice to women in the Church today is a question of the highest moral order."[41]

Back home in Chicago, we continued to reach out to the many women of Chicago. Soyla Villicana, Director of Mujeres: Latinas En Accion met with us in December 1978 to see how her organization and Chicago Catholic Women might work together. We invited Soyla to our board meetings, and we invited Mujeres to participate in our April 7, 1979, conference, featuring a keynote speech, "Do You Know Your Rights?" by Susan Catania, State Representative of the 22nd District and Chairperson of the Illinois Commission on the Status of Women.

---

41 Ibid.

CHAPTER 8
The Baltimore Women's Ordination Conference

The Baltimore Women's Ordination Conference was held November 10–12, 1978, and was titled "New Woman, New Church, New Priestly Ministry." Two thousand women and men attended. The proceedings of the conference recorded the essence of the event as: "To Baltimore came those who were engaging the issues for the first time to the weary and battle-scarred whose sense of urgency and anger increased with each passing day. There were the women who called for ordination now within the present structure and those who spoke of a renewed priestly ministry, not at all achievable within the present structure. There were those who came for support and nurture and others who came for concrete action."[42]

The WOC task force members for the conference were Dolores Brooks, Rose Colley, Maureen Dwyer, Ada Maria Isasi-Diaz, Rosalie Muschal-Reinhardt, Rosemary Kutz, Dolly Pomerleau, Virginia Power, Donna Quinn, Ilma Rosskopf, Sue Secker, Sylvia Sedillo, Elaine Sonosky, Elizabeth Thoman, Lindsay Thompson, Luke Tobin, Marge Tuite, and Barbara Zanotti.

---

42 Maureen Dwyer, Editor, *New Woman, New Church, New Priestly Ministry: Proceedings of the Second Conference on the Ordination of Roman Catholic Women* (Rochester, NY: Kirkwood Press, 1980): 13.

The planners for the Baltimore Conference had asked an ordained priest, Bill Callahan, to lead us in the celebration of a Eucharistic Liturgy. Most of the assembly attended this liturgy. However, in a small room, Barbara Zanotti, one of the WOC task force members, had called women together for a woman-led celebration of the Eucharist. Something divisive and yet wonderful happened in that moment. With all the talk about ordination and women celebrating the Eucharist, we were faced with a dilemma...*which celebration would we attend?* The planners thought that since we had planned for the one male-led celebration that we ought to follow through with that one, but our hearts told us that we loved the one in the other room, woman-led and revolutionary.

After this conference, Chicago Catholic Women held regular liturgies—always women planning and leading the Eucharistic Celebration. Before the conference, women did celebrate together but when such liturgies were reported on, the women never wanted to be publicly pictured. One story pictured women celebrating Liturgy but the picture was darkened so their identities would not be known. It was still a stigma to be a woman celebrating Liturgy!

The President of the NCCB, Archbishop John R. Quinn of San Francisco, declined an invitation to the conference, saying that the Holy See "has clearly taught that fidelity to the apostolic tradition makes it impossible for the Catholic Church to ordain women to the priesthood." He urged instead that attention be devoted to "the role of women in accord with the doctrinal position of the Church."[43] Bishop Thomas Kelly, general secretary of the bishops' conference, criticized the gathering by saying, "The chances of change are minimal—if not non-existent."[44] Alternately, Bishop Nicholas D'Antonio, who was exiled from Honduras and was now vicar general in the New Orleans Archdiocese said, "There is a new Church being born and it will consist of many women." Noting that the number of male candidates for the priesthood was decreasing and that the Vatican had sometimes changed its position on other issues, he added: "Men, let us listen to the women and to the Word of God."[45]

At the Women's Ordination Conference, Patricia Hughes spoke at one session asking the question: *If ordination were permitted now, would I, or would I not be ordained?* This was the question of the moment. It seemed to have a hope about it that since ordination was in the immediate future, we had better answer this question. It also harkened back to our original declaration—of the first conference in 1975—that we wanted ordination only in a "renewed priestly ministry." *Did we really want to accept ordination in this patriarchal Church?*

The title Mary Hunt gave to her plenary address seemed to answer that: "Roman Catholic Ministry: Patriarchal Past, Feminist Future." She stated, "The paradigm of Church has shifted from that of a transnational religious corporation based in Rome, to that of a people's Church...the shift involves us in a basic change in the power structure from hierarchical to com-

43 "Archbishop Quinn Declines Invitation to Conference, *The National Catholic Register*, 19 November 1978.
44 Ibid.
45 *The Chicago Catholic*, 24 November 1978.

munal.... No longer is clerical, celibate hierarchical ministry adequate to the pastoral needs of our day."[46]

Elisabeth Schussler-Fiorenza brought a stark reality to the discussion by saying Rome's "Declaration on the Question of Admission of Women to the Ministerial Priesthood" verged on heresy. She said,

> If women had thought requests for ordination, based on the accumulated research of theologians as to the scriptural and moral justification for female priesthood would eventually be recognized as a just cause...we were mistaken.
>
> If we had thought that arduous scholastic preparation of unprecedented numbers of seminary women would demonstrate our capabilities...we were mistaken.
>
> If we thought that the example of Latin American women ministers filling in for the priest shortage, administering parishes in barrios, struggling against poverty and oppression was living witness to a desperate need in the church...we were mistaken.
>
> If we thought that our work in ministerial roles would, through the concerted efforts of our brothers, change at the local level...we were mistaken.[47]

Participants affirmed recommendations, calling for the following:

---

46 Maureen Dwyer, Editor, *New Woman, New Church, New Priestly Ministry: Proceedings of the Second Conference on the Ordination of Roman Catholic Women* (Rochester, NY: Kirkwood Press, 1980): 32.

47 Chicago Catholic Women, *UPDATE*, December 1978.

- A nationwide boycott of church collections until full membership in the Church was extended to Catholic women. Money should instead be diverted to women's ministries.
- Establishment of a task force to facilitate the inclusion of lesbian and gay men in the public ministry of the Church.
- A Strike Day in April to dramatize the subordination of Catholic women in the Church. Women should be absent from any Eucharistic Liturgy at which a male priest presides.[48]

Elisabeth Schussler-Fiorenza encouraged participants to limit their attendance at Eucharistic services to three times a year. This "spiritual hunger strike" would be difficult for women who were very dedicated to the Church. The sacraments were primary nourishment. "How could we go on without them? But the suffragists who fasted didn't find it easy."[49]

---

48 *Chicago Tribune*, 13 November 1978, Section 1:12.
49 Ibid.

CHAPTER 9
The Equal Rights Amendment

The Vatican had announced the death of Pope Paul VI on August 6, 1978. He was 80 years old when he died and will always be remembered for his "Declaration on the Question of the Admission of Women to Ministerial Priesthood" that he had issued in January 1977. The all-male Conclave of Cardinals elected Pope John Paul who took the names of his two predecessors. He held that office for 34 days before his death. He will always be remembered for this prayer, attributed to him: *God is our Father but even more so, our Mother.*

The all-male Conclave of Cardinals returned to Rome after the death of Pope John Paul on September 28, 1978. The Cardinals broke with a tradition of four and a half centuries by electing a man who was not Italian. Their choice was Karol Wojtyla, from Poland, who at 58 was the youngest pope in over a century.[50]

While the all-male Conclave of Cardinals was celebrating their election of Pope John Paul II, Chicago Catholic Women was celebrating the bill extending the time for ratification of the Equal Rights Amendment. The extension passed the House of Representatives in August and the Senate in October 1978 giving us three more years—from March 22, 1979, to June 22,

---

50 Thomas Bokenkotter, *A Concise History of the Catholic Church* (New York: Image Books, 1979): 14.

1982—to work on passing it. It was March 22, 1972, when the Equal Rights Amendment passed from the U.S. Senate to the states for ratification. Thus began a decade of campaigning for this change to the Constitution.[51]

Illinois would be key to this movement of states to ratify the ERA, which read:

1. Equality of rights under the law shall not be denied or abridged by the U.S. or by any state on account of sex.

2. The Congress shall have the power to enforce, by appropriate legislation, the provisions of this article.

3. This Amendment shall go into effect two years after the date of ratification.

From its beginning, Chicago Catholic Women worked for the passage of the ERA. In its October 1975 newsletter, it highlighted this as an important issue of social justice.[52] In June 1976 newsletter, *UPDATE* noted, "The ERA rally in Springfield on May 16 was attended by Chicago Catholic Women. Helen Sauer Brown addressed the rally from a mother's perspective and Marilyn Uline represented Women Religious for ERA. Beth Wagner and Donna Quinn were also on the platform for the issue."[53] In 1976 the NCCB Bicentennial Recommendations listed the passage of the ERA in two of its sections

51   Chicago Sun-Times Features, *Illinois Women: 75 Years of the Right to Vote* (Performance Media, 1996): 19.
52   Chicago Catholic Women, *UPDATE*, October 1975.
53   Chicago Catholic Women, *UPDATE*, June 1976.

(Personhood and Work).

—✿✿✿—

From November 18 to November 21, 1977, Virginia Gorsche and I traveled to Houston, TX, for the first national meeting for women's rights since the Seneca Falls convention in 1848. This was called by the United Nations and titled "Women on the Move." What a wonderful experience! There were women from all countries of the world, together with women from all over the United States. What I particularly shall never forget were Susan Catania, Illinois State Representative and delegate to the conference, breastfeeding her youngest of eight daughters on the floor of the assembled body; marches for gay and lesbian rights; and just tremendous energy focused on passing the Equal Rights Amendment.

Gloria Steinem wrote: "For myself, Houston and all the events surrounding it have become a landmark in personal history, the sort of milestone that divides our sense of time. Figuring out the date of any other event now means remembering: Was it before or after Houston? I had learned, finally, that individual women could be competent, courageous, and loyal to each other. Despite growing up with no experience of women in positions of worldly authority, I had learned that much. But I still did not believe that women as a group could be competent, courageous, and loyal to each other. I didn't believe that we could conduct large, complex events that celebrated our own diversity. I wasn't sure that we could make a history that was our own...But we can. Houston taught us that."[54]

Because of the Sinsinawa Dominican Religious Community to which I belonged, I had a notion of women as a group being competent, courageous, and loyal to each other. I also had been part of the National WOC Conference in 1975 and was just as amazed with the outcome of the NCCB National Call to Action Conference in 1976. But Houston was my first experience of a government-sponsored conference for women's rights.

As Lindsy Van Gelder remembered in a later *Ms.* article: "Houston transformed us all...We formed and fortified dozens of networks that will live beyond Houston and help implement the Plan (recommendations of the conference), from a new national coalition to help battered wives, to an organization of feminist elected officials, to a continuing caucus of American Indians and Alaska natives. And most of all, we learned that the slogans and rhetoric of our movement are moored in concrete human experience. That sisterhood is powerful. That we are everywhere. That we shall overcome. And that failure is impossible."[55]

—❀❀❀—

In May 1978, the bishops met again at the Palmer House hotel. One important agenda item was their vote on the ERA. I

---

54 Gloria Steinem, *Outrageous Acts and Everyday Rebellions* (New York: Simon & Schuster), excerpted in *Ms.: Celebrating Feminism—The First Century,* "'77 First National Women's Conference," December 1999–January 2000, Vol. X, No. 1: 67.

55 Lindsy Van Gelder, "The Women's Conference," *Ms.: Celebrating Feminism—The First Century,* December 1999–January 2000, Vol. X, No. 1: 68.

remember being invited to speak to a group of nurses about pastoral care the same morning that the bishops were discussing the ERA. I said to this group of nurses that even as we spoke, the bishops were voting "Yes" to the ERA. I was so certain it would pass the Administrative Committee of the NCCB. Alas, I spoke too soon. I left the meeting with the Nurses Association and headed over to the bishops' meeting at the Palmer House; I could hardly wait to hear the good news. As I approached the first floor lobby of the Palmer House, I saw a circle of people I knew. In their midst was Marge Tuite sadly listening to Bishop McManus of the Administrative Committee. He had tears in his eyes as I joined the group in the lobby. He told me that the NCCB Administrative Committee voted "not to vote" on the issue of the ERA. I couldn't believe what I was hearing—I had been so sure! I must have stood there in disbelief for several seconds. *Why did I ever believe in them? They would never take a public stand for women.* We had worked so hard; and this would have meant so much to women from the Catholic tradition and to our work for its passage in Illinois.

The ERA did not pass. To make it part of the federal constitution, 38 states needed to ratify it. We had 35 states. Those states that had not ratified it were Alabama, Arizona, Arkansas, Florida, Georgia, Illinois, Louisiana, Mississippi, Missouri, Nevada, North Carolina, Oklahoma, South Carolina, Utah, and Virginia.

Illinois was the only state in the nation requiring a 3/5 margin to pass it. Rallies were held. Women like Maureen Fiedler and Sonia Johnson had fasted in Springfield for days before the vote in Illinois was taken.

Chicago Catholic Women joined with other groups in an ERA economic boycott of states that had not ratified the ERA. The spring 1978 convention of the NCEA (National Catholic Educators Association) would be held in St. Louis and Missouri had not ratified the ERA. NCEA officials would not change the location of the convention, so we sent word out to teachers in Catholic schools to boycott the convention...but to no avail. The meeting took place; our time had run out.

—❀❀❀—

The Equal Rights Amendment failed to pass the two-thirds majority required for passage in Illinois by June 1982. The ERA was not ratified. By 1983 men were still paid more than women even though the Equal Pay Act of 1963 required equal pay for men and women with the same jobs. The U.S. Department of Labor reported that in 1981 "waiters make an average of $200 a week, while waitresses earn only $144."

CHAPTER 10
Responding to Racism, Sexism, and Anti-Feminism
in the Seventies

Chicago Catholic Women was honored on February 20, 1977, by the Association of Chicago Priests. This was at ACP's Annual Awards and Fundraising Party held at Niles College, 7135 N. Harlem Ave., at 7 p.m. I accepted the award and ended with a thank you to our God: "May She continue to bless us." Laughter and clapping filled the hall. Laughter because this was not typical practice to call God a feminine name; the clapping to show their approval.

This whole evening was a moving one for my brother, Bill; my sister, Joyce, who had flown in from Denver to be there for me; and me because our dad had died just a month before this award was presented. We certainly felt his presence and pride as he shared this evening with us in a new way.

I couldn't help but think of a story about my dad from 1966, the summer Martin Luther King marched through Marquette Park. My brother was assistant pastor at a parish near there. The parishioners were very upset with this civil rights demonstration in their midst, and my brother stood up against this form of racism. On the evening before the march, there was a parish meeting to discuss the event. Before the meeting, my dad, brother, and a priest friend had dinner together. The friend said that the anger had reached such a pitch that there might be guns brought to the meeting that my brother was chairing. Bill was going to listen to the people but not back down on his stand against racism. My dad said good-bye to Bill after dinner. That night, Dad walked into Bill's meeting, put his coat on a chair in the back of the room, and took a seat, unbeknownst to my brother. Many people in the parish knew my dad and loved him. They started to come over to him, greeting "Mr. Quinn." His presence seemed to take the edge off the anger and hatred they felt. Hopefully, both his and my brother's courage changed some hearts because the meeting ended peacefully.

That courage was needed as we continued our work on racism in the seventies.

—❀❀❀—

The 1977 school year brought busing to Chicago Public Schools to achieve integration. It was a volatile situation. On September 16, 1977, I attended a meeting at the headquarters of Operation PUSH (Jesse Jackson's People United to Serve Humanity) in Chicago to gather information on the state of desegregation busing. I also represented Chicago Catholic Women at the Leaders of Chicago meeting held at the Amalgamated Meat Cutters-Department of Civil Rights. On September 21 I was part of a meeting at St. Mark's Methodist Church on 84th and St. Lawrence to be in ecumenical dialogue with the Ministers of Chicago.

The Sisters of Mercy published an open letter to the people

of Chicago regarding the discrimination against our children. I supported their letter and went with other nuns to form a circle of protection for the children at the Stevenson School at 80th and Kostner. A group of us got there for the school's dismissal and boarding of the buses at 3 p.m. and I couldn't believe what I saw. There were women dressed as nuns with long habits and masks on their faces. The real nuns that I stood with were all in regular clothes. We had not worn habits in ten years. The other women who were dressed in long habits and veils whipped out cigarettes and began smoking as if to make fun of those of us who were standing there, continuing their ridicule of nuns. They shouted at us to go home and back to our apartments. I stood there in disbelief. As the young African-American children came out of school to board the buses, they looked frightened with these people screaming at them to stay out of their neighborhoods. That was a day I will never forget. A day I was not proud of my beloved Chicago.

— ❀❀❀ —

One of Chicago Catholic Women's first projects was to collect data on the exclusion and discrimination of women in Archdiocesan and parish structures and to present a viable model for Affirmative Action to improve the position of women in the Catholic Church in Chicago. In 1974 men made an average of $3,433 more than the average earned by women; and for every dollar a man made, a woman earned 59 cents.

In 1974, Affirmative Action was defined as any measure that

seeks to correct or compensate for past or present discrimination and to prevent such discrimination from happening in the future. Numerous laws at the state and federal level called for equal opportunity and affirmative action on the basis of race, color, national origin, sex, religion, age, disability, and veterans' status. The laws were The Civil Rights Act of 1964; Title VI, Title VII, and Title IX of the Education Amendments of 1972; the Equal Pay Act of 1963; the Age Discrimination in Employment Act of 1967; the Rehabilitation Act of 1973; and the Vietnam Era Veterans' Readjustment Act of 1974. The Illinois Human Rights Act prohibited discrimination on the same bases as federal law, and the Illinois Constitution stated that equal protection under the law shall not be denied or abridged, by the state or its units of local government and school districts, on account of sex. The Illinois State Board of Education in 1986 required each school district to have a written policy on sex equity. In 2015, sexual orientation has been a recent focus of justice efforts both in city policy and in the state.[56]

In 1974, Chicago Catholic Women, being concerned about women's representation in Archdiocesan offices, made contact with Catholic Charities, the Catholic Television Network of Chicago, the School Board, the Office for Divine Worship, and the Center for Pastoral Ministry to study the role of women in these agencies. We sent a questionnaire to these agencies, asking:

- Does your agency have a written affirmative action pol-

---

56 Illinois Now, "Affirmative Action: The Facts" (information page), 1986.

icy and program? May we have a copy? If no, are you open to developing one?

- Have any steps been taken to analyze the situation of women in your agency? What were the results?

- Would you describe the basic structure of your agency and the involvement of women at each of the levels? How are personnel for the above recruited and selected?

- Are the compensation and benefits for men and women occupying the same position equal?

- Do you have someone responsible for equal employment opportunity and fair employment practices in your agency? May we meet with him/her?

A Chicago-based organization, Women Employed, had advised us on our approach, encouraged us to predicate our final program summaries on statistics. We focused on the organization Catholic Charities since we knew they received federal monies and would have to comply with federal regulations regarding affirmative action policies. Catholic Charities granted us an interview and responded with this: they had six administrators—all priests; a 21-member executive committee—all male; and a fundraising board of 280 men. Much work needed to be done to change this.[57]

I wrote a letter dated March 23, 1976, to Monsignor Holbrook, the Director of Catholic Charities, on behalf of Chicago

---

57 Catholic Charities, Archdiocese of Chicago, "Organization Chart of Catholic Charities of the Archdiocese of Chicago," 1974.

Catholic Women, thanking him for our interview with him and for the materials he presented.[58] A follow-up interview was requested of the Program Director, Mr. James Carson. During this interview held on April 7, 1976, by Marie Nord and Virginia Gorsche, Mr. Carson stated that a new organizational chart was at the printers and that it showed seven of 15 department heads were women—up from zero women in 1973. He said that each department developed its own objectives and goals for upgrading personnel, and each department was responsible for turning in a quarterly register that the committee evaluated annually.[59]

—❀❀❀—

Advancements for women were made slowly over the years. By 1994, twenty years after we started asking questions of Archdiocesan agencies regarding women, Illinois NOW released a statement that women with high school diplomas earned 68 cents for every dollar made by a man with the same educational attainment. Among college graduates, it was 69 cents for women for every dollar made by a man. An M.A. degree earned women 1 cent more, or 70 cents for every dollar earned by a man. That was one cent's worth of advancement for every degree. Still, women in 1994 held 45% of management jobs, compared to 27% in 1980, and 52% of all professional jobs, compared to 47%

58 Donna Quin, for Chicago Catholic Women, Letter to Monsignor Holbrook, Director of Catholic Charities, 23 March 1976.
59 Marie Nord and Virginia Gorsche, Representatives for Chicago Catholic Women, Interview of James Carson, Affirmative Action Program Director of Catholic Charities, 27 April 1976.

in 1980. Women-owned businesses were increasing at twice the rate of male-owned businesses. And women of all ethnic backgrounds now graduated from college at rates higher than men. NOW attributed this rise in women's presence in work and universities to Affirmative Action.[60]

There was still a ways to go in 1994: Men were 80% of the members of the U.S. House of Representatives, 90% of the U.S. senators, 99.9% of professional athletic team owners, 97% of school superintendents, and 100% of past and current U.S. presidents.[61]

$$-\text{❀❀❀}-$$

We always knew when our message hit "home" (or hit the Vatican) because we would soon hear some negative message about women from Vatican City. In the late seventies, it was the word *feminism*. The Associated Press reported from Vatican City that "Pope John Paul II urged nuns not to allow *feminist* claims to overshadow their call to a chaste, poor, and obedient life in the Church. He said they should always dress in a fashion clearly indicating their religious state."[62]

The article went on to say, "The Pope's speech came four days after a meeting of American nuns and laywomen in Baltimore (our second Women's Ordination Conference) demanded admission to the all-male priesthood and an enhanced role for women in the Roman Catholic Church."[63]

---

60 Illinois NOW, "Affirmative Action: Who Needs It" (information leaflet), 1995.
61 Ibid.
62 Associated Press, *Chicago Sun-Times*, 17, November 1978.
63 Ibid.

With this response, the new Pope, elected on September 28, 1978, only two months before the Baltimore Conference, was making sure that all women knew he would not support their effort to rid the Church of sexism. He would further show that he did not understand the movement behind feminism in his effort to divide nuns and laywomen.

Rosemary Radford Ruether translated for CCW's newsletter *UPDATE* an article titled *Papal Anti-Feminism* written December 3, 1978, by Porfirio Miranda, a Mexican Liberation Theologian. This was one of several articles written on women in relation to the conference of Latin American bishops in Puebla, Mexico (January 28–February 12, 1979). "John Paul II begins to show his colors as a supporter of the reactionary line when he attacks the Feminist Movement. Now is the time for Catholics of the Left to reflect on these matters, that is to say, those who take the Gospel seriously."[64]

The article continued, "The Pope has said to women that the feminist demands are irrelevant. And so, with a levity that is incomprehensible to an intellectual, he has tried to undermine and discredit the global feminist movement. The feminist demands are no more than the affirmation of equality *vis-a-vis* males. What could be more just, more Christian, and a more unobjectionable cause than this?"

"The Pope exhorts the nuns to take the proper line in this matter. Has he taken the trouble to inform himself even superficially, about these things that he is rejecting with all the weight implied by his office? It seems to me that this is not the case.

---

64 Chicago Catholic Women, *UPDATE*, February 1979.

This reinforces for me the contrast that he purports to draw between St. Catherine of Siena and the feminist movement. Catherine of Siena (1347–1380) was one of the most independent and rebellious women who has ever existed in history. For years she poured out incessant criticism of European society. Kings, Popes, and Emperors never were able to dominate her. They feared her more than any other person of her time. From the biographies of the saint that I have read and the histories of the fourteenth century that I know, it seems to me solidly supportable that if St. Catherine of Siena were living today she would be the President of the world feminist movement! Certainly few persons who live demonstrate in so forceful and powerful a manner as she, the equality of women with men, which is the fundamental claim of the feminist movement. So how is it that women should reject the feminist movement and imitate Catherine of Siena."[65]

This Pope had only to read the studies of two well-known groups in theological circles, the Catholic Theological Society of America and the Catholic Biblical Association of America, to know that the arguments used against women's ordination by the Vatican and the National Conference of Catholic Bishops were no longer valid.

A research team of the Catholic Theological Society of America countered the claims that women should not become priests because:

1. All of Jesus's twelve disciples were men.
2. Mary, the Mother of Jesus, was not one of the twelve.

---

65 Ibid.

3. The tradition of a male priesthood is consistent with "the constant practice of the Church."

4. The Scriptures uphold the role of men as heads of the household of faith.

5. The priest, in celebrating the Eucharist, fulfills the symbolic role of Christ and must, therefore, bear a "natural resemblance" to Christ.

6. Men and women have a complementary relationship, women being equipped by nature for some roles and men for others.

Anne Carr, Sara Butler, Margaret Farley, Edward Kilmartin, and Frederick Crowe, members of the research team of the Catholic Theological Society of America stated that instead of stressing "obedient docility to the past," shift focus instead to "God as operating in the eternal now, and therefore still exercising sovereign freedom with a range of options open." As for "constant practice," the researchers said that in recent years the Church has changed its rules governing ecumenical dialogue and the role of bishops, "Is there not a precedent here for change on the role of women in the Church?"[66]

After a three-year study, another group, the Catholic Biblical Association of America, issued a statement in its quarterly publication stating that the New Testament "points toward the admission of women to priestly ministry." The seven members who made the study were Madeline Boucher, Fordham University; Richard Dillon, St. Joseph Seminary, New York City; John

---

66 Roy Larson, *Chicago Sun-Times*, 28 May 1978.

Donahue, Vanderbilt University; Elisabeth Schussler-Fiorenza, University of Notre Dame; Eugene Male, Mt. St. Mary's Seminary, Norwood, OH; Sandra Schneiders, the Jesuit School of Theology, Berkeley, CA; and Richard Sklba, St. Francis Seminary, Milwaukee. They went on to say in the study, "the claim that the intention and the example of Jesus and the example of the apostles provide a norm excluding women from priestly ministry cannot be sustained on either logical or historical grounds." After examining the role of women in early Christianity, they concluded:

1. The New Testament evidence does not indicate that one group controlled or exercised all ministries in the earliest Church.

2. Women were members of the earliest community, which formed the nucleus of the church, and were among those who received the Spirit at Pentecost. Ministry, which derives from the gifts of the Spirit communicated by baptism, was open to women.

3. In the New Testament there are no texts which address the specific question of women and Church office.[67]

---

67 Roy Larson, *Chicago Sun-Times*, 12 December 1979.

CHAPTER 11
Pope John Paul II Visits the U.S.

One year after his election, Pope John Paul II decided to visit the United States. His itinerary would begin September 29, 1979, with visits to Boston on October 1, the United Nations on October 2, Philadelphia on October 3, Des Moines on October 4, Chicago from October 4 to 6, and Washington D.C. from October 6 to 7.

Chicago Catholic Women sent a letter dated August 23, 1979, to the Pope, welcoming his visit in the spirit of hope that he would address the issues of sexism that were prevalent in our Church. The letter included the following:

> We were given much hope in that one of your first visits as Pope was to the Church of St. Catherine of Siena in Italy to recognize the leadership of Catherine in the Church of her day. We are confident now that as we enter this year of the sixth centenary of St. Catherine's death that you will address the people and Bishops about the need for this same courageous leadership by women in our Church.
>
> A Church that is truly an empowering body will recognize the gifts of women for preaching, and will promote the full participation of women in the life and ministry of

the church by eliminating sexist language and sexual discrimination in Church law and liturgical practices and will ordain women to the ministries of our Church.

Finally, we ask that your words to us, when in English, not include sexist terms as *all men, mankind,* etc., but rather reflect a conscious effort to include women in words as *humankind, all people,* etc.[68]

By September 7, 1979, the Vatican issued a directive that no women may assist in distributing Holy Communion at Masses conducted by Pope John Paul II during his U.S. tour. Only priests, deacons, and acolytes—orders open only to males—were being enlisted to help distribute Communion at papal masses.

Women, as well as non-ordained men, had been permitted since 1973 to assist in distributing Holy Communion as "special ministers of the Eucharist." However, this was only allowed when there were not enough priests to distribute Communion promptly, particularly in large parishes. The common practice, however, was to regularly schedule women to be Eucharistic Ministers at weekend liturgies.

It was easy to see why the directive that no women may assist in distributing Holy Communion sent by the Rt. Rev. Msgr. Virgilio Noe, the pontiff's Master of Ceremonies, was causing much anger and perceived as another way to keep women at a distance. It was also easy to understand that the next step for Chicago Catholic Women was for us to call for a boycott of the

---

68 Donna Quinn, for Chicago Catholic Women, Letter to Pope John Paul II, 23 August 1979.

liturgy to be celebrated in Grant Park by the Pope and more than 350 U.S. bishops.

With the cost of this Grant Park liturgy running over one million dollars—while Catholic schools were being closed all over the city due to lack of funds, women banned from assisting as Eucharistic Ministers, and people shouting *clericalism*, it is no wonder the *National Catholic Reporter* on September 21, 1979, reported my statement on behalf of CCW, saying it was "an affront to all people, but especially to women, who are prohibited from orders because of their gender. We sincerely wonder if the Pope knows of this insult. If he does, we hope he will spend some time while in the U.S. talking with women's groups and learning their perspective."[69]

For the Chicago visit of the Pope, Chicago Catholic Women had called for participation of women as Eucharistic Ministers during the October 5 Grant Park Liturgy. When that was denied, we called for a boycott of the Liturgy, and finally, we requested a meeting of the Pope and women's organizations during his visit in the United States. None of these were granted or responded to by the Vatican.

CCW sent a statement to Pope John Paul II; Most Reverend Jean Jadot, Apostolic Delegate to the U.S.; the Cardinals of the U.S.; the leadership of the NCCB; and the media:

> Roman Catholic women in the United States are outraged by the recent Vatican directive that forbids women to distribute the Eucharist during liturgies celebrated by Pope

---

John Paul II. The action is evidence of the institutional Church's continued policy of discrimination against women participating in the full life of the Church.

Roman Catholic women are tired of a clerical leadership that demeans their dignity and refuses to acknowledge that "every type of discrimination...based on sex...is to be overcome and eradicated as contrary to God's intent." *(Vatican II—Gaudium et Spes #29)*[70]

As the media contact for CCW, I was inundated during the Pope's visit with media calls. They were coming in from all over the United States and out of the country. It seems unbelievable now, but try as I did no one in Chicago was available or felt she was capable or prepared to talk with members of the media. I learned how to talk with the media out of necessity rather than formal training. Although I had gone to some training sessions for development work, and had taken a course in public relations, there was nothing like being thrown into what was at hand. I could not back down, I always felt I was representing not only Chicago Catholic Women but all women in our movement. I often had to shake off shyness and make myself respond as best as I could, reminding myself that it was always bigger and more important than myself.

Joe O'Brien, President of the Association of Chicago Priests, sent me a letter dated September 24, 1979, saying, "I honestly do think you and the other leaders have done a super job of gaining media attention and interest. Many men and women are encour-

---

70 Vatican II documents.

aged by the stand you've taken. It's not easy to judge what practical tactic is best at this time, but I do share your concern. I hope you drew strength and support from all your friends yesterday, even if things were hectic with TV cameras, etc."[71]

Then, a most wonderful thing happened in Washington, D.C., on October 7, 1979. The Pope visited the Shrine of the Immaculate Conception to speak to the religious of the diocese. Women inside gathered in one place and wore blue armbands to signify their solidarity. The President of the Leadership Conference of Women Religious, Theresa Kane, was asked to make her remarks to the Pope and all gathered there, including her mother, Mary; her sister Rose; and her niece Mary Beth. What happened there was a moment of truth, courage, and one remembered for all time.

Theresa had what none of us could experience—a few minutes of the Pope's attention in a public audience, speaking for all women. She very respectfully welcomed him in this shrine dedicated to Mary, the Patroness of the United States and the Mother of all humankind.

> It is appropriate that a woman's voice be heard in this shrine and I call upon Mary to direct what is in my heart and on my lips during these moments of greeting.
>
> I welcome you sincerely; I extend greetings of profound respect, esteem, and affection from women religious throughout this country. With the sentiments experienced

---

71 Joe O' Brien, President, Association of Chicago Priests, Letter to Donna Quinn, 21 September 1979.

by Elizabeth when visited by Mary, our hearts too leap with joy as we welcome you—you who have been called the Pope of the people. As I welcome you today, I am mindful of the countless number of women religious who have dedicated their lives to the Church in this country in the past. The lives of many valiant women who were the catalysts of growth for the United States Church continue to serve as heroines of inspiration to us as we too struggle to be women of courage and hope during these times.

Women religious in the United States entered into the renewal efforts in an obedient response to the call of Vatican II. We have experienced both joy and suffering in our efforts. As a result of such renewal, women religious approach the next decade with a renewed identity and a deep sense of our responsibilities to, with, and in the Church.

Your Holiness, the women of this country have been inspired by your spirit of courage. We thank you for exemplifying such courage in speaking to us so directly about our responsibilities to the poor and oppressed throughout the world. We, who live in the United States, one of the wealthiest nations of the earth, need to become ever more conscious of the suffering that is present among so many of our brothers and sisters, recognizing that systemic injustices are serious moral and social issues that need to be confronted courageously. We pledge ourselves in solidarity with you in your efforts to respond to the cry of the poor.

As I share this privileged moment with you, Your Holiness, I urge you to be mindful of the intense suffering and pain which is part of the life of many women in these United States. I call upon you to listen with compassion and to hear the messages of our Church addressing the dignity and reverence for all persons. As women we have pondered upon these words. Our contemplation leads us to state that the Church in its struggle to be faithful to its call for reverence and dignity for all persons must respond by providing the possibility of women as persons being included in all ministries of our Church. I urge you, Your Holiness, to be open to and respond to the voices coming from the women of this country who are desirous of serving in and through the Church as fully participating members.

Finally, I assure you, Pope John Paul, of the prayers, support, and fidelity of the women religious in this country as you continue to challenge us to be women of holiness for the sake of the Kingdom. With these few words from the joyous, hope-filled prayer, the *Magnificat,* we call upon Mary to be your continued source of inspiration, courage, and hope: *May your whole being proclaim and magnify the Lord; may your spirit always rejoice in God, your Savior; the Lord who is mighty has done great things for you; Holy is God's Name.*[72]

The Pope sat in silence, not smiling, not welcoming these words, spoken with the firmness of St. Catherine herself. There was a silence broken by the clapping and cheering of women heard around the globe. Media people were heard to say that

---

72 Theresa Kane, Address at the Shrine of the Immaculate Conception, Washington, D.C., 7 October 1979.

they were at lunch, caught off guard, thinking that nothing more would happen and that this would be a wrap-up today with the Pope heading back to Rome. They scrambled to telephones and press rooms filled with typewriters to report the biggest event of the Pope's visit. This wonderful woman named Theresa spoke from her heart what was in our hearts.

This was what I like to call *a moment in time*. It can never be repeated. It will be there for all eternity for future generations to see. It will define us, comfort us, inspire us, and always be there for our generation to savor, ponder, and direct our future actions.

We must not forget the women from Washington, D.C., who organized and planned to stand inside the Shrine of the Immaculate Conception that day, wearing their blue armbands. We must not forget the woman from Des Moines who said, "He is surrounded by men. How can he ever know how women feel?" We must not forget another woman from Des Moines who tried to receive Communion from the Pope in her hands but he would only place the host on her tongue.[73] We must not forget the women in Philadelphia who heard him repeat that ordination is only for men because God intended things to be that way.

After the Pope's visit, 180 Catholic academics of the Greater Chicago Area released a statement on November 12, 1979, registering their "regret" over "the vision of the Church" presented by the Pope during his visit to the United States. They objected to his "vision of a monolithic church" and his "closed model of

---

73 *Davenport Messenger*, 11 October 1979.

hierarchical authority." They stated that "the Catholic Church is one of rich diversity, of pluralism, not only in terms of ethnic heritage, but also in terms of critical opinions." The statement went on to say, "We do not regard this diversity as a threat to truth, but rather the authentic means by which to discover fuller truth. We find the vision of a monolithic church incompatible both with the best of our experience and also with the inspiring vision of human rights and the dignity of persons enunciated by the Pope in his message to the world. This closed model betrays the ideal of religious liberty not only for the American experience but also for the rich diversity of the Catholic tradition." They concluded their statement with an appeal to the Pope to "be open to dialogue with critical Catholic thought on these important issues."[74]

Chicago Catholic Women issued a statement to the media that said, "The message of Theresa Kane was clear—and this has been the goal of Chicago Catholic Women since 1975: full participation of women in the ministries of the Church. We had hoped for a miracle that John Paul II would dialogue with women in the U.S. His speaking presence without a listening presence to the concerns of women in the Church is not encouraging. More than anyone else, women have taken seriously the message of social ministry as articulated by Pope John Paul II in the U.S. and Yankee Stadium. The ecclesial conservatism of his message to change structures in society which oppress must also be made to change sexist church structures which oppress. The dignity of each person is a statement about human

---

74 Statement by 180 Catholic Academics of the Greater Chicago Area, 12 November 1979.

rights and justice. It is an act of injustice to all people to discriminate against 51% of the Church, for this is to deprive the whole Church of the richness of the gifts which God has given to women."[75]

— ❀❀❀ —

The Pope's response to his trip to the U.S. was to spend Monday and Tuesday at his retreat center in Castel Gandolfo and then to speak to a group of 600 Italian nuns in St. Peter's Square on Wednesday. He told them they needed to show "firmness and delicacy" in the Church. As he spoke to these superiors of various Italian orders gathered in Rome for an assembly, he continued "Show yourselves above all, mothers, to be sensitive and enlightened, not ever irritated or bitter for nothing...Let you be rather, courageous in a holy manner in following the voice of Christ's vicar in a way that no nun feels depressed or separated, even if she may have erred."[76]

Continuing on this theme of motherhood, the Pope made another declaration on November 7, 1980, attacking the Women's Liberation Movement as contrary to a woman's vocation to motherhood. Rosemary Radford Ruether circulated a brief statement with her cover letter saying, "It seems that our brother, John Paul II, is determined to make himself more and more the enemy of women. I think it is important not to let these opportunities go by, but to use the international platform that he

---

75   *Chicago Tribune*, 12 October 1979.
76   Associated Press, "Pope Asks Nuns to Be Sensible," *National Catholic Reporter*, 10 October 1979.

creates to say something in reply." Her attached statement said,

We feel that the roles of parenting of children in the family are vital to society, but that these are roles of fathers and mothers alike, not of women alone. To reduce woman's identity solely to that of motherhood is to violate that primacy of personhood which the Pope himself has defended in his writings on human nature.

We believe that the Women's Liberation Movement, in its primary purposes, is a just and necessary corrective to the long centuries of subjugation of women to secondary participation in human development. We call upon the Pope to better acquaint himself with the actual concerns of this movement and to enter into dialogue with the women themselves who are the members of this movement.[77]

---

77 Rosemary Radford Ruether, Statement to Chicago Catholic Women and other groups, 7 November 1980.

CHAPTER 12
Organizing Women of the Church Coalition and
Advocating for Inclusive Language

Women of the Church Coalition began in May 1977 with Dolores Brooks, Rosalie Muschal-Reinhardt, and myself, all members of Chicago Catholic Women and Women's Ordination Conference. We called for organizations across the country to come together with our women's agenda. The goals of the Women of the Church Coalition were to create a political base that would bring a Gospel perspective of the issues of racism, classism, and sexism to the institutional Church, and to raise consciousness of women in the Church to the Church's stance relative to these issues.

The following organizations responded to our call: Chicago Catholic Women, Christian Feminists, Institute of Women Today, Las Hermanas, Leadership Conference of Women Religious (LCWR), National Assembly of Women Religious (NAWR), National Black Sisters Conference, National Coalition of American Nuns (NCAN), National Sisters Vocation Conference Priests for Equality, St. Joan's Alliance, and Women's Ordination Conference (WOC).

At the same time, Chicago Call to Action began a Call to Action Coalition. I represented Chicago Catholic Women in this coalition, which met *outside* the Palmer House at an event we were calling a "sidewalk celebration and call to justice."

Inside, the newly formed Women of the Church Coalition rented a room, posted a sign outside the room, and invited the bishops to dialogue with us. Filled with energy, enthusiasm, hope, and youth, we had a two-day program on May 3 and May 4. The notice said, "We invite our bishops and people to reflect with us during the annual spring meeting of the National Conference of Catholic Bishops on the Resolutions on Women passed during the National Call to Action. We will also reflect on the recent Declaration on the Question of the Admission of Women to Ministerial Priesthood. The place is the Palmer House – 6th Floor – Parlor H – State & Monroe."

On Tuesday, May 3, we began with a 9 a.m. liturgy, followed by several hours of testimony and response; from 7 to 9 p.m. we had prayer and a songfest. On Wednesday from 2 to 5 p.m. we had a reflection on the Declaration with Rosemary Radford Ruether speaking on tradition and Elisabeth Schussler-Fiorenza speaking on Scripture. Only two bishops—Lucker from New Ulm, MN, and Buswell from Pueblo, CO—came to the room to dialogue with us. Exciting as it was, we were becoming aware that we had much work ahead of us to accomplish our goals.

Thus began Women of the Church Coalition, which would later sponsor the first Women-Church Conference in 1983.

—❀❀❀—

The next year, in May 1978, the National Conference of

Catholic Bishops deliberately rented every available room in the Palmer House so we could not have a space in the hotel. We had to strategize around this. We learned how to acquire press passes. We made our presence felt by asking questions at press conferences—and talking with bishops in the hallways. Our numbers in the coalition were growing to include not only the founding organizations but also the Catholic Committee on Urban Ministry, Catholic Women's Seminary Fund, Catholics Act for ERA, Center of Concern, 8th Day Center for Justice, Knights of Peter Claver–Ladies Auxiliary, Network, Quixote Center, Religious Formation Conference, Scapegoat, Tabor House, and Women for Dialogue.

After the 1978 NCCB meeting, I, as coordinator of the Women of the Church Coalition (1977–1981), and accompanied by Dolores Brooks and Rosalie Muschal-Reinhardt (coordinator 1981–1984), approached Bishop McAuliffe, Chairperson of the NCCB Committee on the Role of Women in Society and the Church, as he was waiting for a taxi to the airport. We suggested to him that we might coordinate classes to be held for the bishops to educate them on women's issues. We were very serious about this request. He laughed and said they would never come to any classes and especially not on women's issues. (That July Bishop McAuliffe gave testimony in Missouri in favor of the Equal Rights Amendment even though the Administrative Committee of the NCCB at this meeting had voted not to vote in favor of the ERA.)[78]

On November 5, 1979, the Women of the Church Coalition

---

78   *The Catholic Voice*, 21 July 1978.

met in Washington, D.C., and sent a telegram to Theresa Kane while she was in Rome at the meeting of the International Union of Superiors General. The telegram said: "...We applaud you; we especially want to thank you for speaking about the anguish of women in the Church and for using the only opportunity available to communicate it."[79] As coordinator of Women of the Church Coalition, I signed the letter on behalf of the included organizations: Catholic Committee on Urban Ministry, National Assembly of Women Religious, Catholic Women's Seminary Fund, National Black Sisters Conference, Catholics Act for ERA, National Coalition of American Nuns, Chicago Catholic Women, Network Christian Feminists, Quixote Center, 8th Day Center for Justice, Religious Formation Conference, Institute of Women Today, Scapegoat, Las Hermanas, Tabor House, Leadership Conference of Women for Dialogue Religious, and Women's Ordination Conference.

Recall that our first recommendation out of the Bicentennial National Call to Action was that the National Conference of Catholic Bishops, in consultation with a body of representatives of each of the national Catholic organizations of women, establish within the NCCB/USCC an effectively staffed structure to promote the full participation of women in the life and ministry of the Church... and that this representative body design, develop, and implement such a staff structure. The coalition worked to have membership on the NCCB Committee on the Role of Women in Society and the Church. Of course, we were told this was impossible since the committees could only have

---

79 Women of the Church Coalition, Telegram to Theresa Kane, 5 November 1979.

bishops as official members. They did have consultors, however these were women not connected to our coalition. Bishops on the NCCB Committee on the Role of Women in Society and the Church in 1979 were Bishop McAuliffe (Chair), Bishop George Evans, Bishop Amedee Prouix, Bishop Ernest Unterkoefler, Bishop Carroll Dozier, and Bishop Francis Murphy. The consultors were LeMay Bechtold, Kathleen Cravero, Loretta Favret, Edwina LeFils, and Agnes Cunningham.

The coalition met twice a year—once in Chicago and once on the East Coast. We shared our concerns and our organizational agendas and signed our names to endorse needed actions. By 1979, to celebrate our two-year anniversary, the coalition presented a petition to Bishop McAuliffe on Wednesday evening, May 2, 1979. This petition, signed by over 13,000 women and men from Holland, Belgium, Ireland, England, Pakistan, Saudi Arabia, India, and 47 states in the United States, asked the bishops "to pursue vigorously with the Vatican Sacred Congregation for the Doctrine of Faith, the withdrawal of the second argument set forth in the declaration on the question of omission of women to the ministerial priesthood. This argument demeans all women and priests by claiming that male physical sexuality is the fundamentally important element in the priestly representation of Christ."[80]

McAuliffe informed the bishops of the request during a general session and presented them with copies of the petition. There was no open discussion of the issue. Archbishop John

---

80 Bob McClory, "Rousing Vision Now Committee Assignment," *National Catholic Reporter*, 11 May 1979: 6.

Quinn, President of the NCCB, later said it is "most unlikely" that U.S. bishops will endorse the petition. I was quoted as saying "the fact that such concerns are being mentioned aloud at the bishops' meeting represents some reasonable progress."[81] Looking back now I wonder if we were satisfied with too little progress.

Again the bishops were looking outward to injustices, asking if Puebla should serve as a model for a similar conference by the American bishops. "What can we do and what should we do in regard to the policies of our own government, which affect and aggravate the scandalous conditions in Latin America?" asked Bishop Quinn who also called for daring initiatives in light of Puebla. Sexism in the Church was not an issue the bishops wanted to discuss.

By this NCCB Conference in May 1979, the coalition, in existence for two years, had not succeeded in getting representation on the NCCB Committee on the Role of Women in Society and the Church, the bishops to support the Equal Rights Amendment, or the bishops to endorse the petition to have the Vatican retract its statement that a priest must bear a natural *male* resemblance to Christ. To top that list off, for the most part, the section on women from the National Call to Action Bicentennial Conference was wiped out.

What we had gained was more widespread support for women's issues in the Church and more women's organizations springing up locally and wanting to belong to the coalition.

---

81 Ibid.

—❀❀❀—

We were ready to take on another issue—sexist language. Women of the Church Coalition wrote to Archbishop Quinn in a letter dated November 9, 1979, stating that, "The Women of the Church Coalition would like to urge you to encourage your bishops to vote in favor of the Liturgy Committee's proposal to change the sexist language of the Liturgy...We would like to commend Archbishop [Rembert] Weakland [of Milwaukee] for his concern for the pain of Catholic women."

The bishops voted down the Liturgy Committee's recommendation. The Quixote Center initiated an open letter to the Bishops, which was signed by the Coalition, expressing our outrage and regret at their voting.

Chicago Catholic Women worked perpetually on inclusive language. Chicago Catholic Women did not want "too generic" to be an excuse for not using "humankind" over "mankind" or "chairperson" instead of "chairman." It mattered to us that phrases like "manned the booths" be replaced by "staffed the booths."

I criticized the refusal of the nation's Catholic bishops to end "sexist language in the Church's prayers and liturgy," comparing the bishop's action to Peter's denial of Christ at his trial. "Even your speech betrays you," I said of the bishops, paraphrasing Matthew 26:73.[82] The organization repeatedly contacted J.S. Paluch, a Catholic music publisher, about changing songs in

---

82 Jack Houston, *Chicago Tribune*, 13 October 1979.

their song books and encouraging song writers to use inclusive language.

Joan Chittister was the guest speaker of Chicago Catholic Women on April 30, 1978, at St. Scholastica. Her topic was inclusive language. Joan was the past president of LCWR, and had worked with us in Detroit at the National Call to Action Bicentennial Conference. With her doctorate in social psychology and speech communication, she called on Church leaders to use inclusive language. "The failure of the Church to address women as women is effectively to make them nonpersons who need not be dealt with." Dealing with the argument that if the issue is unimportant, it was reported that Joan had suggested that we try to say that "God came to save all women, that we are all daughters of God, and that the Church should be a model of sisterly love. The change should be easy—if it is not really important."[83]

—❁❁❁—

We had 21 organizations belonging to the coalition by 1980. We would come to focus on ordinations, passage of the ERA, and inclusive language. I spoke with Archbishop Weakland regarding the last issue to see what the Liturgical Committee would be presenting at the next meeting in May. He was having the International Committee on English in the Liturgy (ICEL) work on the canons, and he appreciated any materials we could offer on removing sexist language to share with the bishops.

83 Patricia McCormick, *Chicago Tribune*, 19 February 1978.

In February 1981 Rosalie Muschal-Reinhardt became the new Coordinator of the Coalition. By 1982 the coalition decided to have a national conference the following year. This conference would be called "Women-Church Speaks: From Generation to Generation." It was held in Chicago, November 11–13, 1983, at the O'Hare/Kennedy Holiday Inn in Rosemont, IL. The sponsoring Coalition members were Chicago Catholic Women, Institute of Women Today, Las Hermanas, National Assembly of Religious Women, National Coalition of American Nuns, Quixote Center, Women's Ordination Conference, and Women's Alliance for Theology, Ethics, and Ritual. After the conference the sponsoring organizations decided to become Women-Church Convergence and invite groups across the country to be part of this movement.

CHAPTER 13
CCW Moves into the Eighties

In the beginning, it was always a dream of mine to spin the organization off and then be able to watch from a distance while it grew—much like watching a youngster grow into adulthood. I could see this dream starting to take shape when Ann Sipko was given one year to work for Chicago Catholic Women by her Racine Dominican Community. She began working in the office in April 1979.

In August of 1979, we were offered office space at 1307 S. Wabash Ave. for a reasonable rent. We were grateful to 8th Day Center for Justice for giving us space since 1974, but we were growing and found it necessary to move to a larger office. On September 1, 1979, we moved to 1307 S. Wabash, Room 220. While I continued my work as staff person at 8th Day Center, representing the Sinsinawa Dominicans, Anne would work in the new Chicago Catholic Women office. Other groups that worked on the second floor in the 1307 building were NCAN, Institute of Women Today, Association of Chicago Priests, National Federation of Priests Counsels, and Parish Evaluation Program.

At that time our budget covered rent, telephone, printing, postage, supplies, organizational memberships, and speakers' fees, but we were still trying to find a way to do fundraising to support staff salaries. As Chicago Catholic Women's annual budget expanded to $3,100, it was noted in our September newsletter that the Archdiocese had 19 members on its Archdiocesan Finance Committee. All nineteen members of the committee were men—clergy and lay. While women were major contributors to Church collection baskets, not one woman was part of this Finance Committee.[84]

—❀❀❀—

Theresa Kane spoke to the issue at a Leadership Conference of Women Religious on August 24, 1980: "I submit respectfully that the women's issue in the Roman Catholic Church is not, and cannot be, an isolated issue. The exclusion of women from the Church as a system, is a root evil and a social sin, which must be eradicated if women are to be engaged in the institutional Church. I am concerned for the growing number of women who have left the Roman Catholic Church and for those among us, both sisters and laywomen, who can no longer enter into the sacramental life of the Church because of the sin of sexism. When we address the social sins of sexism and paternalism in the institutional Church it is essential to distinguish persons from systems. The challenge to women is to address directly the evils within the systems and yet retain a compassionate stance towards the persons who may be involved either consciously or unconsciously in perpetuating the sinfulness."[85]

84 Chicago Catholic Women, *UPDATE*, September 1979.
85 Theresa Kane, Speech to the Leadership Conference of Women Religious (LCWR), 24 August 1980.

It was the eighties and our work continued.

—❦❦❦—

The Wellington Avenue United Church of Christ came to the rescue of Chicago Catholic Women in February 1982 when everything was set for a fundraising concert by folksinger Kristin Lems. Chicago Catholic Women had everything organized for the evening with St. Sebastian Church, a parish that volunteered to give us space any time. We made arrangements only to be told two days prior to the concert that we could not use their facilities because they had received too many calls from anti-choice people threatening a protest if they let us use their facilities.

It all centered around one line in one song Kristin sang telling of the difficulty an economically poor woman with several children had in making a decision about having an abortion. The song was neither pro-choice nor anti-choice but simply told how this woman was coping with an important decision in her life. We were cancelled at the last minute again. Again, Chicago Catholic Women was safe only on the streets and not in Catholic facilities. And, once again, those of other faith traditions had the courage to take us in.

—❦❦❦—

In March 1982 Chicago Catholic Women lifted up the names of seven members who founded or served in shelters for women and children in the Chicago area: Lois McGovern (Dehon House), Patricia Crowley (Howard Area Community Center), Joanne Halt (The Crisis Center of South Suburbia), Monica Cahill (Taproots), Chris Hannible (Sarah's Circle), and Charlene Kazmierski and Beth Daddio (Siena House).

— ✿✿✿ —

In May 1982 Theresa Kane spoke to Chicago Catholic Women in the home of Patty Crowley. Over 100 people were there to hear her words. In September 1982 Sonia Johnson spoke about her book, *From Housewife to Heretic*, reminding us "that power will not be given; it must be seized." Sonia also reminded us that "as the rhetoric rises, the lid goes down. Language is used to distract us from what is really happening."

— ✿✿✿ —

Many wonderful women served on the coordinating committee of Chicago Catholic Women over the years. The list of board members' names from 1979 through 1985 reads like a Catholic Women's Hall of Fame:

Margaret Dunn

Bernie Smierciak

Madalynn Smith

Marianne Supan

Soyla Villicana

Patty Crowley

Carol Luczak

Carmelita Madison

Lois McGovern

Mary Powers

Ann Sipko

Donna Quinn

Marge Tuite

Maureen Reiff

Marilyn Steffel

Valerie Wojciak

Audrey Denecke

Loretta Finnerty

Marie Walter Flood

Joellen McCarthy

Katie Murphy

Suzana Schlessinger

Rosemary Radford Ruether

Mary Buckley

Barbara Ferraro

Mary Louise Schneidwind

Carole Hegarty

Kay Scharf

Loraine Doane

Kathy Burke

Vera Fina

Paula Basta

Peg Boivin

Susan Catania

Donna Goetz

Suzanne Holland

Elaine LaLonde

Jacquie Wetherholt

Carla Wilde

Mary Jane Jeffries

Ann Benedict

Sheila Daley

Connie Driscoll

Catherine Gallagher

Maureen Gallagher

Sue Secker

Margaret Traxler

At different points during these years, Loraine Doane, Kay Scharf, Dorothy Corrigan, Michelle Wierzgac, and Angie Weiss worked in the Chicago Catholic Women's office answering the telephone, taking in the mail, and keeping the files and address labels updated using the one electric typewriter we had and a fax machine. Angie Weiss reminds me that this was before the age of the computer! We are most grateful to all these women.

— ❀❀❀ —

In March of 1981, the *Chicago Sun-Times* had reported that Cardinal Cody barred Melinda Roper, International President of the Maryknoll Sisters, "from preaching in her home parish in suburban Park Ridge. Her community, with missions in 22 countries, was prevented from occupying the pulpit last Sunday at Mary, Seat of Wisdom Church when Cody enforced a canon law stating that all laity, even religious, are not allowed to preach in the church."[86] The *Tribune* also covered the story, saying that "the text of her remarks centered on the responsibility of the Catholic Church in war-ravaged El Salvador, where four American church-women, including two Maryknoll sisters—Maura Clarke and Ita Ford—along with Jean Donovan and Dorothy Kazel, were killed last fall....Cardinal Cody has been criticized recently by Catholic activists for what they say is his failure to state forthrightly his opposition to United States military aid to the ruling junta in El Salvador."[87]

---

86   Roy Larson, *Chicago Sun-Times*, 25 March 1981.
87   *Chicago Tribune*, 26 March 1981.

In April 1983, Chicago Catholic Women sponsored an evening to honor the four women murdered in El Salvador in 1980. The new video *Roses in December* was shown. We invited the cousin and aunt of Jean Donovan, Erin and Marilyn Murphy, as well as a panel of women from Chicago who were recently in Nicaragua, to give their political analysis and connections between U.S. Foreign Policy and the countries of Central America. These four women would always remain with us.

The Peace Pastoral issued by the U.S. bishops in May 1983 failed to see the connection between militarism and patriarchy. Women of the Church issued an open letter to them in response. The Peace Pastoral, noted our statement, was "issued from a hierarchical and patriarchal base, which excludes women from the fullness of ministry and decision-making. We call on the U.S. bishops to recognize the connection between militarism and sexism. Militarism and patriarchy are inextricably linked because both define relationships in terms of superior and inferior." We were prepared for the release. Chicago Catholic Women organized a visible protest at the bishops meeting on Sunday, May 1 and Monday, May 2, to focus on the sexism rampant in patriarchal systems that inevitably leads to war.

— ❀❀❀ —

Over the years, the National Coalition of American Nuns (NCAN) had received about 650 letters from women who had never before revealed that they were victims of incest. On May 24, 1983, Margaret Traxler, board member and founder of

NCAN, and myself, as president of NCAN, issued a statement about incest that stated, "Men of the Church have preached against adultery and abortion, but why have they virtually ignored [rape and] incest? These women wrote to us because they saw us as Church and trusted us."

The statement from NCAN continued, "While the Church often discusses the female sin of abortion, it does not discuss the male sins of [rape and] incest. With a celibate clergy you run into problems, and when you have women as a non-entity, how do you address these issues? These women wrote to us because they saw us as Church women who could speak out on these topics. One-fifth to one-third of all girls under 16 are survivors of rape and incest and at least two-thirds of adolescent prostitutes, adolescent female drug addicts, women alcoholics, and women in federal prison are victims of incest [and rape] attacks."

— ❀❀❀ —

Margaret Traxler, Deb Barrett, Ann Patrick Ware, and I appeared on the Phil Donahue Show in 1982 to discuss a statement issued by NCAN against the Hatch Amendment, which prohibited the use of federal funds (e.g., Medicaid) to cover abortion. The four of us agreed that decisions about abortion should rest primarily with those who are directly and personally involved. In taking this stand, we set ourselves in opposition to the NCCB on the issue of the legislation that the bishops supported. It always seemed that men could make any statements they wanted about being anti-choice but women were reprimanded for their pro-choice statements.

—❀❀❀—

At the beginning of the eighties (and again at the beginning of the nineties), I was called and blessed to share the story of Chicago Catholic Women and to learn of the stories of women in other parts of the world. The first trip was to Peru, Bolivia, and Ecuador. I went with other staff members of 8th Day Center for Justice. We talked with Maryknoll Sisters Rose Dominic and Rose Timothy who worked in the Women's Center and with women on the hillside outside of Lima, Peru. The women of these countries taught me so much. My only regret was not knowing the language well enough to be able to communicate more directly with them.

Fortunately, that was not true for my trip to the Netherlands in the nineties. The Sisters there asked me to make the trip and share our story of the Women's Movement in the U.S. They were so wonderful and showered us with great hospitality wherever we went. They spoke English or translated the stories shared about Chicago Catholic Women and Women Church. They shared their stories of organizing women and their work to change the institutional Church. We were both eager to learn from one another. I would often refer to the women from these countries as great women of courage, compassion, and commitment.

I remain grateful for these travel experiences in my lifetime.

CHAPTER 14
Transitioning from Cardinal Cody to Cardinal Bernardin

In November 1981, the *Chicago Sun-Times* reported that "faced with Cardinal John P. Cody's 10-month refusal to comply with two government subpoenas, U.S. officials are taking an important new attack to discover whether Cody illegally diverted as much as $1 million in tax-exempt church funds for non-church use. Federal grand jury subpoenas have been served on at least five banks in Chicago."[88]

Alongside the newspapers reporting that two leaders of the National Coalition of American Nuns—Margaret Traxler, a member of the executive board, and me, the Coalition President—pressed for thorough investigation of the possible abuse of fiscal power, there were also the responses of Cody's supporters. Archbishop John Roach of Minneapolis-St. Paul and President of the National Conference of Catholic Bishops recommended a "speedy and just resolution" to the allegations: "I can say that my heart goes out to the Church in Chicago and to Cardinal Cody, whom his brother bishops have known for many years and esteem today as a man of integrity...and dedication to the Church."[89]

Reports went on to say, "Cody, 73, received two rounds of

---

88 *Chicago Sun-Times*, 4 November 1981.
89 Press Wire Service, "Church Leaders Seek Cody Probe," *Chicago Sun-Times*, 4 November 1981.

applause during a closed-door meeting with about 65 members of the Priests Senate after concelebrating a Mass at the Senate's meeting at St. Mary of the Lake Seminary in Mundelein, IL. Rev. Thomas Healy, President of the Priests Senate, said the Cardinal made no reference to the controversy, but at the close of the meeting, *Battle Hymn of the Republic* played on the organ and Cody remarked, 'Yes, this is a battle, isn't it?'"[90]

Back on Cody's 70th birthday in 1978, he was interviewed and proudly stated, "There's nobody who's built as many schools in the hierarchy—and I don't want to be bragging about this—in five different dioceses." However, the reason he gave for closing Catholic schools was, "We don't have the money. We don't have the sisters. We can't keep doing the things we did when a sister was getting $50 a month. Today she's wanting to be paid like any other lay teacher."[91] I wonder if that is the reason why nuns now beg for retirement money in every diocese. Twenty years later, we are seeing the fallout of a system that rested on large numbers of women entering the communities and thus "taking care of" or replacing their retired nuns in the workforce. By the early seventies the signs were there. Our generation, who had been through Vatican II, and mothers, who were getting a taste of women's liberation, were not encouraging their children to enter religious life. This, coupled with the many options now opening up for young women, created a decline in women entering communities of women religious.

Cardinal Cody was from a different generation. When tell-

---

90   *Chicago Sun-Times*, 4 November 1981.
91   David Smothers, UPI, *The Denver Post*, 7 April 1978, and *The Milwaukee Journal*, 16 April 1978.

ing stories of his young days in the Secretary of State's Office at the Vatican, he said, "If I thought Cardinal Pacelli [later Pope Pius XII] who was my immediate boss, or Montini [now Pope Paul] was doing something wrong—and I could tell them that; I did so on different occasions, when I was asked—I would do so. But if they said, 'This is the way it is going to be done'...fine. We don't have that today. The concept of authority has taken a nosedive, so authority as such is being downgraded all over. It's a rebellion against authority that goes on in the Church and outside."[92]

Cardinal Cody died on April 25, 1982.

— ❁❁❁ —

As CCW confronted the apparent sexism in the selection process for a new Chicago Archbishop in our media outreach, we cited a talk Pope John Paul II gave to 4,000 priests' housekeepers in the spring of 1982, charging that sexism is "rampant" in the Church. Bob McClory, writing for the *National Catholic Reporter*, related:

> "Twelve members of the board of consultors (all male) select as the interim representative (male), who presides until the next archbishop (another male) is chosen by the Pope," declared a CCW press release. "Any hope for a new approach from Rome is contradicted by John Paul's attitude expressed in his speech to the Domestic Collaboration in

92 Ibid.

the Priesthood who were on a pilgrimage to the Vatican last month.

"Women do have their place in the Church," declared the pontiff. "Be happy that you can keep the residence of the priest clean and free him from material tasks which would absorb part of the time he so needs for his apostolic labors. Such material tasks, said the Pope, are more suited for female charisms...you could never thank God enough for giving you the grace of choosing to serve the clergy."

Chicago Catholic Women called on all Catholics to oppose the degrading sexist attitude which prevails in the Catholic Church...women are doing well in leadership roles in society and can no longer relate to a church which does not recognize them.[93]

The first Midwest Regional Women's Ordination Conference of 1982 met with women from Illinois, Wisconsin, Iowa, and Missouri coming together to discuss their roles in a male-dominated Catholic Community and to celebrate Liturgy. Speaker Marjorie Tuite told the group that it was time for women to begin to plan for changing the Church's system but also that expanding the role of women in the Catholic Church could be a long, slow process. She quoted me when I said, "it was a celebration rather than a confrontation of religious experience for women who broke bread together in celebration of the gifts of priesthood we have through baptism." Marjorie continued,

---

93 Bob McClory, *National Catholic Reporter*, 28 May 1982.

"It is up to individual women participants to decide for themselves if the liturgy was a Mass...We are no longer performing this liturgy in the catacombs or underground but we are going public with this."[94]

At this time, the latest Gallup Poll showed that 44% of U.S. Catholics now supported women's ordination. This represented a significant increase from 1974 when only 29% supported women priests. Dolly Pomerleau, co-director of the Quixote Center, the group who commissioned this series of Gallup Polls, said, "We will see a majority of U.S. Roman Catholics supporting women's ordination within three to five years. When the issue is most publicly controversial, support increases more rapidly; when it is relatively less visible, support continues to increase, but the pace is slower."

It had been almost eight years since the founding of CCW, thinking that in five, maybe 10 years, there would be full equality for women in the Church, made as we were *in the image of God.*

—❀❀❀—

On July 10, 1982—three months after Cardinal Cody's death—Joseph Bernardin was appointed Archbishop of Chicago and was installed on August 25, 1982. Born in Columbia, SC, on April 2, 1928, Bernardin became Archbishop of Chicago at the age of 54. Prior to this he had been Auxiliary

---

94 *Long Island Catholic,* 4 November 1982.

Bishop of Atlanta in 1966, General Secretary of the NCCB from 1968 to 1972, President of the NCCB from 1974 to 1977, and Archbishop of Cincinnati from 1972 until his appointment to Chicago. He was made a Cardinal on February 2, 1983, and remained in Chicago until his death on November 14, 1996.

We knew when Cardinal Bernardin was appointed to Chicago that he was not going to agree with our work for women's rights. While he was President of the National Conference of Catholic Bishops (1974–1977), he worked against the ordination of women. Cincinnati knew it intimately and now we would have that experience.

When Bernardin was installed as Archbishop of Chicago on August 25, 1982, I wrote a letter to him, welcoming him and asking for a meeting with him and various women's groups located in the city. We received no response.

The first occasion I had to see him was at the Sinsinawa Dominican's Founder's Day Celebration held at Rosary College on November 4, 1982. After he spoke, he asked the group of nuns if anyone had questions. There was silence. I remember standing from my seat in the last row to ask when he was going to honor the request of several women's groups to meet with him. There was an audible gasp from the group and he responded that he would look into that. Later, he stood in front in a formal receiving line with Wilton Gregory, who had accompanied him (and as of 2004 is a bishop in Atlanta, GA). When I went up to shake Bernardin's hand, he said that he would meet with us.

The meeting took place at the Chancery Office on January 27, 1983. At this meeting with Bernardin was his assistant,

Jim Roache, taking notes and listening to our questions. The questions centered on a whole plethora of women-specific issues (women in prison, women in seminary, Hispanic women, black women, women in pastoral and religious education ministry, divorced women, alcoholic women, feminization of poverty/homelessness, and incest). Marge Tuite summed up the input given. The cardinal also took extensive notes and said that he would stay in touch with us to continue the dialogue.

CHAPTER 15

A New Code of Canon Law and More Efforts to Close the Altar to Women and Girls

One year into his tenure as Cardinal of the Archdiocese of Chicago, Bernardin sent to every pastor a formal ban on girls as altar servers. The ruling, contained in a letter on liturgical matters, was sent in early July 1983, and stated, "As regards the question of girls acting as altar servers, there are directives from liturgical documents which exclude this practice. I would request that all our parishes follow these liturgical norms." He went on to say, "In particular, I do not want young girls to be hurt in this matter, nor do I wish to diminish their enthusiasm for serving the Church."

Chicago Catholic Women rose up against this ruling. Grand-mothers called CCW to say that they saw no difference between their granddaughters and grandsons serving on the altar. One grandmother from suburban Westchester called our office saying the ruling was "an insult and a putdown. I thought the days were gone when we were only good enough to clean the pews." A young mother from Orland Park said the issue of girl servers has "emotional overtones beyond its surface significance. Serving Mass," she said, "is where young girls get their first realization that the Church is not fair, that it is a male-dominated structure."[95]

---

95 *National Catholic Reporter*, 29 July 1983.

Just a handful of Chicago parishes had female altar servers then. St. Clement was one and John Fahey was the pastor there. He reminded us that "Separate but equal has a very bad history in the U.S. The Supreme Court has said it's intrinsically unfair. Just substitute the words 'black children' in place of 'girls,' and you see what is involved."[96]

On August 1, 1983, Chicago Catholic Women organized a demonstration, with a particular call for grandmothers, on the steps of the Art Institute, where the Vatican Art Collection Exhibit was on display, to protest this move in the wrong direction. Seventy demonstrators showed up wearing armbands and carrying signs reading, "We Want a Church for Our Daughters" and "Equal in the Eyes of God but Not in the Church," and leafleting about the issue of altar servers.

After this demonstration, Cardinal Bernardin looked the other way regarding girls as altar servers. Grandmothers continued to speak out and marched with strength. It appeared that the Cardinal got the message even though the new Code of Canon Law prohibited female altar servers. (Ten years later in the early nineties, 111 parishes in the Chicago Archdiocese had female altar servers.)

—❁❁❁—

The new Code of Canon Law was promulgated by Pope John Paul II on January 25, 1983—twenty-three years after Pope John XXIII announced in 1959 his decision to reform

---

96 Ibid.

the existing corpus of canonical legislation that had been last promulgated on the feast of Pentecost in the year 1917. On June 29, 1980, the printed schema of the whole code was presented to the Pope, who forwarded it to the cardinal members of the commission for their definitive examination and judgment.[97] No women were a part of this final process, which would become the law of the Church to which they belong. Women and men met in Detroit to discuss our response to this new Canon. I remember remarking that since the final judgment was reserved to the Pope, women did not have a chance at equality.

The final copy stated that women would have to be ordained to interpret the Word at Eucharistic Celebrations, but of course according to this code women could not be ordained nor could girls be altar servers. Some changes that officially ended some legal discrimination against women in Church law were:

1. Women could become diocesan chancellors, auditors, assessors, financial administrators, or board members of a seminary. They could serve in various diocesan annulment tribunals or courts and on parish pastoral and financial councils.

2. Husbands and wives should be treated with more parity.

3. Female religious orders were given more administrative autonomy.

---

97 *Code of Canon Law Latin-English Edition* (Washington, D.C.: Canon Law Society of America, 1983): xxvi–xxvii.

But no amount of administrative autonomy prevented the Vatican from venting its anger towards religious communities of women. The rampage of the eighties began with Sister Agnes Mary Mansour, a Sister of Mercy, who was ordered by the Vatican to give up her job or leave the religious community. She was Director of the Michigan Social Services Department. Her job required her to administer state funds for abortion. Detroit's Archbishop Edmund Szoka condemned the funding and Agnes stated that it would be unfair to deny funding to women who could not afford it. She chose to continue working with poor women.

In May 1983 Chicago Catholic Women protested this injustice to Agnes Mary Mansour and to all women by marching in front of Holy Name Cathedral and leafleting passersby about the issues.

— ❈❈❈ —

In August 1983, there was a second meeting at the Chancery of various women's groups in Chicago and Cardinal Bernardin. The Cardinal said that he had given some thought to our last discussion (January 1983) and that just a few minutes before we arrived had met with Bob McClory of the *National Catholic Reporter* to announce that he was going to write a pastoral on women in 1984. We expressed concern over the process, as it was our proposal back in January asking for the creation of a task force *that would create a listening board in the diocese, out of which would flow the necessary information for a pastoral letter on women.* We were told by both the Cardinal and his assistant Jim Roache that though he announced a pastoral letter on women there was no process in place at that time. We reiterated that representatives from our coalition must be included in this process and that the patriarchal system had kept women marginalized for too long.

Altar servers and the ordination of women were also points of discussion. The Cardinal invoked the law as he had done in January when I asked him about his personal thoughts regarding the ordination of women. At this point he became agitated and sternly said, "The problem with you is that you want to hold me captive and say to you what you want me to say." (I did not back down and asked him for a third time in Rome ten years later. His response one decade along was quite different. It seems that we all grow a little with each new encounter.)

As he got up to leave the room, we asked about our next meeting with him, but he deferred to Roache, who said he would be in touch. This group did not meet again. We were busy in the next months with a national conference of women, national elections, and finally dealing with the Vatican's threat to expel some of us.

—❀❀❀—

We were living under the new papacy of John Paul II.

Joan Leonard, a Sinsinawa Dominican, recalled meeting John Paul II before he was Pope at a Philosophy Congress in Switzerland. "We were wearing slacks, and he was having difficulty with that. I could tell," she said. "He tried to ask us about it in a very light, offhand way, saying something like, 'Do all sisters in the United States wear slacks?' I told him that we sometimes did, at least when it was appropriate, on campuses. He didn't seem pleased by my answer. I remember that we were both drinking wine and looking at each other across a small table, when it dawned on me that he simply didn't understand the dynamics of the American Church, much less American women. We were from two different worlds, and we both knew it."[98]

John Paul II tried to cross into that other world when he visited the U.S. in 1979 but found a delightfully strong message from Theresa Kane.

"He thinks of nuns as a servant class," quipped Rosemary Radford Ruether, "He brought nuns with him to Rome to cook for him. All his statements about women have only one thing to say: motherhood." "The joke went around" said Suzanne Hiatt, an Episcopal priest, "that he had been told he should step on the ground and kiss the women, and instead he kissed the ground and stepped on the women."[99]

In a letter addressed personally to the bishops of the United States and dated June 24, 1983, Pope John Paul II announced that "he named Archbishop John Quinn of San Francisco to head a special commission to facilitate the pastoral work of the bishops in reaching out to the more than 150,000 men and women religious in this country." Named to assist Archbishop Quinn were Archbishop Thomas Kelly, O.P., of Louisville and

---

98   Otto Friedrich, reported by J. Madeleine Nash (Chicago), "Women: Second-Class Citizens?" *Time*, 4 February 1985: 62–63.
99   Ibid.

Bishop Raymond Lessard of Savannah.

Archbishop Quinn noted that the religious in the U.S. have been engaged in an intensive period of renewal since 1966 when Pope Paul VI gave the religious throughout the world a mandate to update and rewrite their constitutions. He stated: "Now with the submitting of constitutions and the promulgation of the new Code of Canon Law, this unique time of experimentation is ending. But with the ending of the period of special experimentation, the Pope has asked the American bishops to enter into the process in order to support and to second the efforts of the religious to strengthen and to renew their communities."[100]

So, our male leaders thought Vatican II and the sixties and seventies had been "a unique time of experimentation" and that it was "ending"!

---

100 Ibid.

CHAPTER 16

Birthing a Conference, a Convergence, and a Movement Called Women Church

Women of the Church Coalition had decided it was time to have a national conference to tell our stories, do the analysis of those experiences, and move to future action. We wanted to make the connections between classism, racism, and sexism with specific focus on areas of spirituality, sexuality, and survival. We wanted a conference to reflect the experience of women of all colors, speaking different languages, and to cross all generations. We as women wanted to name and claim ourselves as Church. And so in 1982 we began planning a national/international event and named it "From Generation to Generation: Women-Church Speaks." This was the first time we named ourselves: Women Church.

We booked the O'Hare/Kennedy Holiday Inn in Chicago for November 11–13, 1983. Maureen Reiff was chosen as Coordinator of the Conference, assisted by Joanna Sizeck. They would work out of the Chicago Catholic Women office, which gave its space to coordinate this effort. The purpose of the conference was twofold: to bring women together for building "Women Church" and to build networks among women of diverse and similar backgrounds so that we might be and express *Women of the Church*.

The gathering "was designed to deal with Catholic women's concerns as they arose in the context of a history of deep, faithful living. The participation of black, Hispanic, U.S., Third World, economically disadvantaged, physically challenged-women, and women who have distanced themselves from the institution for personal or structural reasons would be invited...The Coalition hopes that the meeting will be an occasion for reconciling women with each other through the hearing of stories, the reflection on theological and ministerial concepts, prayer and celebration, and concrete planning for ways that diverse groups and individuals might better be Women Church in the world."[101]

As the cardinal in Chicago at that time, we had asked Bernardin to contribute to our conference. Bernardin wrote a letter to the Women-Church Speaks Conference indicating that he could not financially support the conference because he did not agree with the philosophy of some of the sponsoring groups, and a donation would be conceived as condoning. We asked him if he would tell us which of the groups he did not agree with, and his quick response was the Women's Ordination Conference.

The activities for the conference included major addresses and workshops with small group interaction and caucuses, celebration and prayer throughout, displays of women's art, space for organizations to share information about their work, entertainment, ethnic foods, opportunities for networking, and child care, with special programs for the children.

On Friday evening we anointed each other at round tables where we sat as equals. Theresa Kane and Elisabeth Schus-

---

101 Women of the Church Coalition, Proposal for 1983 Conference.

sler-Fiorenza left to attend a meeting of the U.S. bishops who were planning a pastoral letter on women. Magda Enriques of Nicaragua came to speak of her testimony to the U.S. Congress against U.S. intervention in Nicaragua. The ritual meal was planned by Diann Neu and was similar to a Seder meal. Marsie Silvestro's music, "From Generation to Generation" filled the room. Rosemary Radford Ruether at her Sunday morning homily called the sexist structure of the Church, military, and government "the idol of patriarchy." Maureen Fiedler stressed our need to analyze the Church as a political institution as it is a human creation. Jesus challenged religious authorities and so must we.[102]

The conference was a resounding success. Over 1,500 women, men, and children came to listen and tell their stories. Women of the Church Coalition, founded in 1977, had birthed a movement and a convergence that would later come be called Women-Church Convergence. Representatives of the Women of the Church Coalition that sponsored the conference were Chicago Catholic Women, Institute of Women Today, Las Hermanas, National Assembly of Women Religious, Quixote Center, National Coalition of American Nuns, Women's Ordination Conference, and Women's Alliance for Theology, Ethics, and Ritual.

I was honored to give the welcoming address to those in attendance; Aurora Camacho de Schmidt translated into Spanish. In the speech, I reported on the scholarships to 100 women totaling $8,000; gave thanks to the 125 women who were part of the program and process; gave thanks to the assembly of

---

102 Donna Goetz, Chicago Catholic Women, *UPDATE*, May–June 1984.

1,500 from 37 states and as far away as Alaska, Canada, London, and Lima, Peru; and remembered those who have gone before us or could not be present among us that day because of illness or caring for those who are ill.

Furthermore, I said: "This is a most critical time in history to have such an event. Now more than ever we as women must tell our stories. The stories of those women who have gone before us on the picket lines; in the factories; in country, town, and city. The stories today of the women demonstrating at the Plaza de Mayo for those who have disappeared in Argentina; demonstrating at Seneca Falls for Peace; the stories of mothers, sisters, friends who hold their wounded and dead in an ever-growing militaristic society; the stories of our sisters who carry everything they own in a bag; and those of our venerable older sisters who will decide between food and heat in the coming months. These are times when men want to own and control—be it small nations, poor people, women's bodies. Yes, these are the times when men want to own and control—be it entire Religious Communities of Women, one woman who gave 30 years in a Religious Community to her ministry, or the altar where our young daughters gather."[103]

After the conference, Women of the Church planners met in Chicago to go over what we learned. We met again in Washington, D.C., and invited other groups to join us. Energized by the positive outpouring of the 1,500 women in attendance at the conference, we decided to continue a coalition that we

---

103 Donna Quinn, Opening Address and Welcome, Women-Church Speaks Conference, 11 November 1983.

would call Women-Church Convergence. The convergence was distinct from the Women Church Movement. While the convergence might sponsor future conferences, the Movement was now worldwide. It moved on its own.

CHAPTER 17
1984–1985 and the Ad in *The New York Times*

The women of Garret Evangelical Theological Seminary (in the near north lakefront suburb of Evanston) organized a protest when Cardinal Bernardin visited there on January 25, 1984. The protest concerned the treatment of Roman Catholic women by the Roman Catholic hierarchy. Considerable controversy erupted at the school, with many finding the demonstrations inhospitable.

Rosemary Radford Ruether, a professor at Garret responded:

> ...[I]n the last two years, there has been a concerted campaign of repression against Roman Catholic Women, especially in American Catholicism, from the Vatican. This has taken the form of harassment of women's religious orders and efforts to repeal their renewal movements; of efforts to remove women both as students and as faculty in Roman Catholic Seminaries; and to repress any discussion of these issues by laity, priests, religious, and even by bishops. Bishops who do not toe the line on this are being "investigated."
>
> The protest against these policies by Roman Catholic Women has been going on for some time, and is mounting...Some might think that Roman Catholic Women may

protest in this way, but it is "unecumenical" for Protestant Women to do so. This seems to me an inadequate concept of ecumenism. To label such a protest "inhospitable and intolerant" is a mystifying and repressive use of these terms. It mystifies the fact that the primary inhospitality that is going on is the inhospitality of the Roman Catholic Magisterium toward Roman Catholic Women, and the primary intolerance that is going on is the intolerance of discussion...within Roman Catholicism.[104]

—❀❀❀—

By March of 1984, Chicago Catholic Women began its Lenten Series with Clare Wagner and Georgene Wilson as facilitators. We continued our monthly Liturgies on Sundays, and by October we were excited about the possibility of having a woman as Vice President of the United States.

I once spoke at an indoor rally for Geraldine Ferraro at Mundelein College. Ferraro took the podium later and, toward the end of her speech, Coretta Scott King entered the auditorium, approached the stage, and greeted each one of us who were up there. I can remember being so excited to greet Coretta that when she approached me I instinctively gave her a big hug to thank her for everything she meant to us. She was quite stiff in her response and I remember thinking that was the wrong thing for me to have done to someone of her stature.

Ninety-seven women and men signed a full-page ad in the

104 Chicago Catholic Women, *UPDATE*, January–February 1984.

New York Times on October 7, 1984, in the midst of the election-campaign dispute over abortion between Democratic and Catholic Vice-Presidential candidate Geraldine Ferraro and New York's Archbishop John O'Connor. The ad declared, "A diversity of opinions regarding abortion exists among committed Catholics." It went on to ask the bishops to facilitate a dialogue on the issue. It was partially a response to Archbishop O'Connor's request to the Archdiocese of New York made on June 24, 1984, urging them not to endorse the Mondale-Ferraro Ticket. "I don't see how a Catholic in good conscience can vote for a candidate who explicitly supports abortion," he was quoted as saying.[105]

The Vatican's response to the ad was a letter from Jean Jerome Hamer, head of the Vatican's Congregation for Religious and Secular Institutes dated December 18, 1984. The letter was sent to the 13 congregations of nuns, and to the bishop and/or president of the male communities. Twenty-four nuns and four priests and brothers had signed the ad. "The Sacred Congregations for Religious and Secular Institutes charged that the religious signers were 'seriously lacking in religious submission and must publicly retract their view or be dismissed from their orders.'"[106]

It was another example of the Vatican trying to influence the political process in the United States. We had only asked for dialogue but yet one more time this was denied us. The Vatican

---

105 Julia Lieblich, *Sisters—Lives of Devotion and Defiance* (New York: Ballantine Books, 1992): 136.
106 Otto Friedrich, reported by J. Madeleine Nash (Chicago), "Women: Second-Class Citizens?" *Time*, 4 February 1985: 62–63.

would again try to silence Catholic women.

The priests and brothers retracted almost immediately. All 24 of us nuns refused to take back our statement. The signers and presidents of the religious communities met at the Fullerton Cenacle (a retreat center) in Chicago on a bitterly cold day in January 1985. The signers not belonging to religious communities were not invited to this meeting, thus replicating the intent of the Vatican to divide women into those who were nuns and those who were not.

This kind of ultimatum had never happened to so many nuns at one time. Many of the presidents of our communities had not studied the issue of abortion and felt at a loss as to their response. After the nuns consulting with canon lawyers, all the signers and the community leaders tried to have a strong and common response to the situation and agreed to meet again in Washington, D.C.

After Washington, D.C.'s, meeting of 35 nuns and lay signers, a statement was issued: "We are appalled by the recent action of the Vatican against women who are members of religious orders. We believe that this Vatican action is a cause for scandal to Catholics everywhere. It seeks to stifle freedom of speech and public discussion in the Roman Catholic Church and creates the appearance of consensus where none exists. A consensus on any issue in the Church cannot be imposed."

Those of us who were part of religious communities received many letters of support from our other members. The Sinsinawa Dominicans had been engaged in women's issues, as had a Sinsinawa Justice Committee, since the mid-seventies, so they showed a great deal of strength in supporting me. There were 28 sisters who said that if I was dismissed they would leave with me.

Many letters between the presidents of the communities and the Vatican ensued. Since Hamer and the Vatican would not communicate directly with the signers, only with the presidents of their orders, Mary Ann Cunningham, a Sister of Loretto, sent a letter directly to Hamer and enclosed her picture with the sentence, "This is what a signer looks like."

On August 21, 1985, Jean Jerome Hamer, a Belgian Dominican, Prefect of the Vatican Congregation for Religious and Secular Institutes, and now with the title of Cardinal as a reward for his disastrous work against religious communities during 1984 and 1985, came to Holy Name Cathedral in Chicago to speak to the men and women of area religious communities.

It was a warm day. No coats were needed. Chicago Catholic Women organized a demonstration in front of the Cathedral. Young girls and women held signs which read "We are all Poped out," and a forever favorite of mine: "We Want a Church for Our Daughters." It was Marion Donnelly Welsh, a longtime CCW member and mother of four daughters, Mary Alice, Lynn, Kathleen, and Janet, who originated this declaration. Everyone wore black armbands. Many of the nuns who went in wore them signifying that the Church was dead for women.

After Hamer spoke in the church, we went over to the auditorium to introduce ourselves and to say a few words to him. I left my armband on but I saw nuns removing them as they waited in line to talk with him. He spoke with each one individually, but then he started scrutinizing what we were wearing, pulling at someone's sleeve, for instance, and asking someone else why she was wearing a pink dress. The insinuation was that we were not in habit.

All at once I remembered that I would be the only signer of the *New York Times* ad who would speak to him, as he would not deal with us but only with the presidents of the communities. I quickly memorized the four points that I wanted to make to him. I got up to him and told him my name and said that I was one of the signers of the ad. At that moment one of the demonstrators, a young woman and member of Chicago Catholic Women, came up a side aisle to the front and took our picture. He became enraged and started running after her to try to grab her camera saying that he had said, "No pictures." She was young and ran faster than he did, and out the front door with her excellent camera. He came back to me shouting that I had organized the whole demonstration outside of the church.

I reminded myself that I stood there for all the signers and would not let this deter me from what I wanted to say. So I began to tell him that I too was a Dominican and "wouldn't Dominic want us to work with poor women who were victims of rape and incest?" I got as far as *Dominican* and he started shouting that I was not a good Dominican and I ought to become one. I continued with my second point that I worked with poor women in a shelter and… I got as far as *poor women* and he shouted that it was time for me to learn what a good nun really is.

He was quite tall so I was looking up at him the whole time and thinking, *this is not going too well.* I started seeing black spots in front of my eyes and realized that if I fainted now I would fall at his feet. And this I did not want. I was determined I would stay upright until I had finished what I wanted to say. My last point was to ask him if he would meet with the signers. The signers would never have this opportunity to ask him, so I wanted to do it for them. He could hardly respond, he was so livid. He face was turning red and his arm went up and he was saying, "I'll give you a meeting. You...you come to Rome. I will give you a meeting." By now I couldn't believe what I was hearing. This was my first experience with a man from the Vatican. I left him and walked across the front of the auditorium but I knew I was going to faint. Strangely, I did not want the other women to see me do that as it would look like a sign of weakness. I guess I wanted to be strong for all of us.

My face must have been as white as my dress and Bernardin was standing in front, several yards away from Hamer. Folding chairs were in the first row. Bernardin came over to me and asked me to sit down. He said, "That man. Do not listen to him." I sat down but I could not talk. I naively thought that nicely asking for a meeting with Hamer would result in one. I honestly did not know that a priest from the Vatican could be so evil.

It was not until April 17, 1986, that a letter was sent from Jerome Hamer of the Vatican's Congregation for Religious and Secular Institutes to the president of our community, Cecilia Carey, stating that there was closure on my case. On May 30, 1986, Cecilia Carey sent a letter to the Sinsinawa Dominicans stating this closure.

After this encounter with the Vatican, I decided to immerse myself even deeper in advocating for women's reproductive autonomy. Everything about the Vatican's response to our signing of the ad in *The New York Times* only served to strengthen my belief in women's right to control over their own bodies, even if that included choosing an abortion. The Vatican had long tried to control our minds and, now, their control over our bodies was losing with the majority of women and me.

Big male donors must have been beating down the doors of the Vatican to do something, while the males at the Vatican continued to stomp on the bodies of those women who were parenting the next generation for the institutional Church. It all makes for interesting "bed fellows." The Vatican will not allow priests or nuns to run for public office while it as an organization lobbies all over the world and especially in the U.S. for the Republican anti-choice platform. Again the old adage feels true: *Do as I say, but not as I do*. And, if I might add: *Most of all do not have a creative thought of your own…and do not think that as women you can have any say at all.*

There is a reason for the shortage of vocations, lack of support, and a falling off of numbers for the institutional Church with each new generation. Women birth the children, women raise the children, and women instill in the next generation their feelings toward the Church. If women have been dismissed, not listened to, not welcomed to the sacred orders of the Church, not welcomed to interpret Scripture such as preaching a homily, not welcomed to serve on the altar during Eucharistic Celebrations, not welcomed to give their input to the laws and policies of the Church, such as Canon Law, and their young sons and daughters are survivors of pedophiles, what response would you *expect* women to have toward such a group that calls itself Church? The next Pope should be a woman, but will the all-male College of Cardinals vote for a woman? I doubt it.

—❀❀❀—

By 1984, I no longer held the romantic notion that Chicago Catholic Women would somehow survive on its own and become fully funded and staffed. The office was staffed during the Women-Church Conference and after that we had the help of two seniors, Loraine Doane and Kay Scharf, who came in to help with mailings and telephone calls. I made the decision to leave my employment at the Business College, located in the same building as CCW, and became the full-time Director of Chicago Catholic Women. This meant I would be the person to do fundraising for staff, overseeing programs, outreach, media work, and continuing to infuse life into the organization.

CHAPTER 18
1985–1986: Spirituality…Sexuality…and Survival

My brother, Bill, suggested that I go over to the shelter at 65ᵗʰ & Woodlawn, St. Martin de Porres House of Hope, in the Woodlawn neighborhood, because Connie Driscoll and Therese O'Sullivan were doing wonderful things there for the women and children in need. Connie had spoken with Bill and priests at other parishes a few months earlier asking for financial help for this shelter. Sister Margaret Traxler and I went over to House of Hope and met the women who lived there. It wasn't long after that visit that I began working with the women, counseling and teaching a class. I also paid visits to the 11-story Chicago Housing Authority building for seniors across the street. Margaret opened up shelters in another part of the South Side while I focused on the House of Hope.

Once connected to St. Martin de Porres House of Hope shelter, I focused in on the women's great need for employment. If we just gave an apartment to a woman and her children after she left the shelter, she would soon be out on the street again if she did not also have employment. The senior women living across the street needed younger hands to do cleaning, cooking, laundry, and grocery shopping for them, and the younger shelter women needed work. I put the two together and wrote grants for funding this program. Thus began CCW's Job-Training Program.

I wrote a curriculum for the Job-Training Program, which included the work and care the shelter women gave to the seniors living across the street at a CHA building. That program was called ElderCare. We published a flyer with pictures and news about our work in the CHA building. We had music programs for the seniors and continued to clean and cook for them. As time went on, great friendships formed between the younger women in the Job-Training Program at the shelter and the seniors living in the CHA Senior Building across the street.

We ultimately had four women employed to run this program: a director, a woman who taught classes, a woman who coordinated the effort with the seniors, and one who coordinated the employment search. They were excellent workers and we continued these programs for the next 15 years through 2000.

In the nineties, our work focused more on getting employment for the women at the shelter after they completed their work with the seniors and our on-site supervisor, Mary Hill. Mary is a terrific woman who worked for us for 15 years. We offered weekly classes with a trainer, who taught classes on such topics as Caring for Seniors, Caring for Children, Making Nutritious and Healthy Meals, Managing an Apartment, Money Management, Interviewing for a Job, and Finding Employment. Women who served as trainers over the years were Ruth Ann Miller, Mary Pat Johnson, Laurie Brink, Cindy Chadwick, and Sarah West.

After eight weeks of classes and assisting the seniors across the street, we hosted a Graduation Ceremony with speeches, music, cake, pop, and a lot of tears of joy. The women marched in to the taped music of "Pomp and Circumstance." They each received a diploma that they proudly showed to future employers at job interviews. For some of the women, this was the first program they had ever completed. They invited family members and, of course, their children were invited so they could be proud of their mother graduating and think about the day when they too would graduate from high school or college. Chicago Catholic Women was proud to see these women leave the shelter, have employment, and have the ability to make a home for themselves and their children. We graduated about 60 to 75 women a year. It was one of our greatest works.

During those years the women at House of Hope made baskets—Easter baskets, birthday baskets, baby baskets, graduation baskets. We sent out flyers asking for donations to purchase the baskets. The women learned how a small business worked and what it took to make, advertise, and eventually market their baskets. We invited the Chicago Catholic Women membership to write poems that we then published in two small books of poetry. We also made meditation beads with a book to accompany them. Donations received to buy these items also went to the Job-Training Program.

—❀❀❀—

In the mid-1980s, CCW saw the need for a coalition in Chicago to work on teen pregnancy. We pooled resources, including material goods to meet the physical needs of the women, funding sources, referral information, and education for the public about such needs. By 1986 we were working to help high schools in the Archdiocese be more aware of the need to change attitudes about young women who wanted to stay in school while pregnant.

Chicago Catholic Women called together this coalition of other organizations to discuss what was being done in the area of teen pregnancies and related issues. The organizations were Bridging, Catholic Charities, Courage, Gehring Hall, Taproots, The Cradle Society, St. Martin's House of Hope, and St. James Care & Courage. We called the coalition Generations.

—❀❀❀—

Not only were members introduced to those of other groups, we still routinely held educational programs alongside our monthly liturgies, with discussions covering topics such as affirming life and pro-choice, report on Nicaragua, sheltering the homeless, and caring for the elderly. In June 1985, Jeanne Hurley Simon and Theresa Kane spoke to our members.

We continued our Scholarship Fund for women interested in furthering their studies in ministry. We prepared to celebrate our ten-year anniversary, where we would rejoice over the past ten years and hail the beginning our next ten years. At our Anniversary Luncheon held on November 16, 1985, Chicago Catholic Women honored women for each year of its existence:

1974, 1975	Donna Quinn
1976	Margaret Traxler
1977	Marjorie Tuite
1978	Rosalie Muschal-Reinhardt
1979	Theresa Kane
1980	Maura Clarke, Ita Ford, Jean Donovan, and Dorothy Kazel
1981	Sonia Johnson, Maureen Fiedler, and Susan Catania
1982	Ada Maria Isasi-Diaz
1983	Agnes Mary Mansour
1984	Patricia Crowley
1985	Rosemary Radford Ruether and Carol Marin

—❀❀❀—

The weekend of November 14–15, 1986, Chicago Catholic Women cosponsored a conference with the Feminist Theological Coalition of Chicago Seminaries, McCormick Women's Concerns Committee, and the United Campus Christian Ministry at the University of Chicago. The conference was held at the University Church in Hyde Park and was called "Spirituality...Sexuality...and Survival." The conference was very well received by women of all faith traditions because of the following discussions: Beverly Harrison spoke on "Sexual Ethics for Today," Mary Hunt spoke on "Friendship, Love and Trouble: A Catholic Lesbian Feminist View," Fran Kissling spoke on

"Pro-Choice Theology," and Rosalie Muschal-Reinhardt spoke on "Spirituality & Sexuality ...One and the Same?"

—❀❀❀—

In 1985 and 1986, the U.S. bishops attempted to write a pastoral on women. Peg Boivin chaired Chicago Catholic Women's response. A brainstorming session was held on October 6, 1985, at Patty Crowley's home. Sue Secker and Sheila Daley took notes and transformed these notes into *Chicago Catholic Women's Testimony for the Proposed U.S. Bishops' Pastoral.* It was presented at the Archdiocese of Chicago hearing on November 9, 1985, by Peg Boivan. Following are the notes in their entirety:

We strongly recommend that the pastoral not be written for several reasons:

1. The bishops are an inappropriate group to be writing an authoritative teaching document on women since they lack, by definition, the human experience and expertise that are only possible from women themselves. Indeed, for male bishops to attempt to articulate women's role in church or society only reflects the patriarchal worldview and ecclesiology which presumably the pastoral was intended to alleviate. In fact, such an action is an expression of the problem—namely, an all-male Church leadership, which

has both structurally and theologically excluded the subjugated women, and now presumes to define what women's contribution should be.

2. To write a pastoral on women is to misconstrue the moral issue which needs to be addressed. Women, as half or more of the membership of the church, are not a moral issue but rather their degradation and oppression are.

3. Finally, the consequences of the bishops issuing such a pastoral would be both pastorally and politically disastrous. Pastorally, it would further the marginalization of many faith-filled women and risk drastic increases in their exodus from the institutional church. Politically, it would undermine the credibility of the American Catholic episcopate or social justice issues both internally and externally. It could foster the impression that the pastoral was, from its inception, solely intended as a vehicle for the re-issuing of offensive patriarchal church views on sexuality, anthropology and theology, since to proceed with writing such a pastoral, in the face of widespread and mounting pressure against it, cannot help but engender this conclusion.

We recommend that instead of writing a pastoral on women, the bishops continue a listening, self-educating process regarding the injustices effecting women ecclesiastically and societally. The issues involved in such a pastoral ought to be no less carefully researched than those on nuclear arms or the American economy. We also recommend that patriarchy and sexism be the topic of a future pastoral. Some of the signs of sexism in the institutional Church that women have pointed out and which need close examination in any formal statement on patriarchy and sexism are:

i. The absence of women in decision-making positions or processes of the Church, in its sacramental leadership, in the formulation and final definition of Church teaching—noting here that the "observer" status of women at Vatican II has been replaced at subsequent synods by no status at all.

ii. Serious and honest reflection must be done on some of the inconsistencies in the Church's approach to abortion and its concern for human life. Some of these inconsistencies are:

   a. Disproportion of financial and other church resources committed to the issue of abortion as compared to such moral evils as rape, racism, nuclear weapons, etc.

   b. The fact that there is no outcry against birth control which the church appears to consider to be as intrinsically evil as abortion.

   c. There is no aggressive effort to address

the financial and moral responsibility of males for engendering life, whether in or outside of marriage.

d. When, as a vice-presidential candidate, Geraldine Ferraro took essentially the same position with regard to abortion as did Edward Kennedy in his campaign, she met with quite a different response on the part of officials of the Church.

e. The failure to seriously address the pastoral aspects of the abortion question, e.g., rape and incest (it should be noted here that two out of five girls fifteen years and younger are presently victims of incest and by age 25, 25% of women have been raped).

f. The fact that in a moral decision which ultimately can only be made by a woman, the moral stand of the institutional church has been formulated exclusively by men.

g. The fact that of all the moral issues that have been heatedly discussed in our society over the last several years, it is the only one on which the church has explicitly stated there can be no dissent.

iii. For many women, the issues of church structure, sacramental leadership, and patriarchal theological and anthropological beliefs are central to the contemporary crises. The situation demands basic re-definition of theology and reformulations of ecclesiology in the light of advancing anthropological and theological insights. Short of that, raising lesser issues is only avoiding the real problem.

iv. We believe that a carefully done listening process will lead the church to reject the January 1977 statement, the Declaration on the Question of the Ordination of Women to the Presbyteral Ministry, as a crude expression of sexism. The church will become aware that there is no shortage of vocations, but only a failure to listen to the Spirit.

We must claim again the right to dissent even from pronouncements of the magisterium, when in conscience we recognize that they represent not the expression of the Spirit, but of a culturally conditioned attitude which implies, even if it does not explicitly state, that women are "misbegotten males" (St. Thomas Aquinas). When we feel compelled to express such dissent, it is not out of hostility to the church, but out of concern for its future.

We are conscious that we are demanding courage from our brothers, the bishops, on this issue. We know some will respond by saying, "but I am committed to communicate to you the teaching and discipline of the magisterium of the Church."

We ask, by whose law? Would you have defended the torture and unjust taking of life by the Inquisition? Would you have defended slavery? You have been eloquent in calling our society to examine the evil and injustice that exists in the nuclear arms race and in our own economy. If you are not equally courageous and eloquent in confronting the injustice within the institutional church, these other statements lose their credibility. We recognize that the current attitude of the Vatican will not be very receptive to such self-examination. For the sake of our daughters and our sons, we pray that you will see yourselves more as an advocate for the experience of the church in this country, than as a representative of Rome.

Additional issues to be addressed in a pastoral on Patriarchy and Sexism:

1. Language and symbols in the liturgy, texts in the Lectionary and Sacramentary which exclude women in a derogatory manner
2. Ordination of women
3. The difference in financial compensation received by men compared to women in church ministry
4. Lack of financial support for women to study theology and prepare for ministry
5. The perception that bishops are not supportive of the contributions of women religious.
6. The tactic of using more traditional and noncritical women's groups as "representative" groups of women and other more critical groups as "angry women." In

this way women are used against women and those who are alienated because of divorce, disillusionment, or sexual preference are no longer "counted" as Church women.

CHAPTER 19
1986–1987: Lifting up the Lives and Works of Women

In our 1986–1987 "season," Chicago Catholic Women continued our educational programs while paying tribute to the works of women. On September 3, 1986, we had a book signing evening with Rosemary Radford Ruether and her new book, *Women-Church*. The copies of her book she graciously autographed went quickly. We had a Valentine's Day party featuring author Mary Jo Weaver signing copies of her new book *New Catholic Women: A Contemporary Challenge to Traditional Religious Authority*. For Lent we invited Joan Leonard to give a talk titled "Biblical Feminism and the Contemporary Woman."

We expanded our Liturgies to every Sunday of the month: the first Sunday was held at St. Xavier College on the far Southwest Side; the second Sunday was in the south suburbs; the third Sunday was at the downtown home of Patty Crowley and Sister House on the West Side; and the fourth Sunday was at Paula Basta's home.

— ❀❀❀ —

We learned through our coalition network in the Spring of 1986 that Mary Ann Sorrentino was excommunicated from the

Church because she worked as the Director of Planned Parenthood of Rhode Island. Her daughter was to be confirmed but had to undergo a grilling on the subject of abortion before she would be permitted to receive the sacrament. Sorrentino received support from the women around her. Her pastor had forbidden her the Eucharist during mass, so she sat in the pew while others went up to receive Communion. But this was not to be denied her. Her supporters would take turns going up to receive Communion (in their hands), taking it back to Mary Ann to share it with her. Again, it was the women giving comfort and hope. CCW's letters to the editor went out for Mary Ann Sorrentino.

—❀❀❀—

Marge Tuite and I had a special friendship. Having said that, I am sure that everyone who knew Marge would say the same thing! Marge and I always met at Christmastime to have dinner and talk about the season, laugh, and talk seriously about the issues. We would exchange gifts and toast the New Year. The last gift Marge gave to me was a pair of candle holders she brought back from El Salvador, which I still treasure.

Marge came to the spring meeting of Women Church Convergence, April 12–13, 1986, in Chicago and remarked to me how thin she was getting. That was the last time I saw her. She went into a hospital in New York and I called her there and spoke with her before leaving for our Sinsinawa general chapter meeting in June. When I learned of her death on June 28, 1986,

I was stunned and saddened. Dolores Brooks, Sue Secker, and I flew out to New York for her funeral. It was at St. Dominic's Church where she grew up. Jack Shea was the celebrant, and I will always remember the pastor announcing at Communion that only those who were Catholic should receive. We sat behind very good friends of Marge who had also come from Chicago and were of other faith traditions. I felt so embarrassed, sad, and angry about this. All should have been welcomed at our table. We would have our own celebration of Marge's life in Chicago, and that we did.

On July 13, 1986, we celebrated Eucharist in Marge's honor at St. Thomas of Canterbury Church on the North Side of Chicago in Uptown. What a great celebration it was. Over 300 people, "the folks" as Marge would say, came to pay tribute to a woman who gave her life to so many—black, brown, and white; women, men, and children.

Her name, "Marjorie," "Marge," "Margie," was also known and loved by the people of Nicaragua, who called her to the priesthood of the people. "Reverend Margie" they chanted as they held candles in a plaza in a Managua barrio during one of her last visits to them. Her memorial service in Chicago reflected the saddened eyes of the adults and children she loved so well. They carried the bread of life, the Eucharist, to all in attendance as we remembered her in the breaking of the bread. If ever I was called to lead a Celebration, this was it. Yes, we were paying tribute to a woman who was a priest—called by the people, ordained by the church of the faithful, and commissioned by the Spirit to lead, prophesy, and live out a full life of justice and love. One who generously said, *This is my body, this is my blood* and gave her life for the poor. Marge encouraged us, *Don't forget the dream... Do this in memory of me.*

— ✿✿✿ —

Though Chicago Catholic Women had lost a friend, we continued on with a new board for the 1986–1987 year:

- Ann Benedict
- Yvette Bryant—Chair of Stopping Apartheid Committee
- Joanne Cullen—Co-Chair of Central America Committee
- Sheila Daley
- Connie Driscoll—Chair of Finances Committee
- Catherine Gallagher
- Maureen Gallagher—Chair of Mary's Pence Committee
- Geraldine Gorman—Chair of Peace & Disarmament Committee
- Fran Koval—Chair of Scholarships Committee and Chair of Legislative & Reproductive Rights
- Lillie Pang—Co-Chair of Pregnant Teens Committee
- Darlene Noesen—Co-Chair of Central America Committee
- Donna Quinn—Chair of Membership
- Beth Rindler—Chair of Liturgy, Ordination, Preach-

ing Committee

- Sue Secker
- Ruby Taylor—Co-Chair of Pregnant Teens Committee
- Margaret Traxler
- Susan Walker—Chair of Lesbian Rights

We were able to give scholarships for ministry training to Marilyn Steffel and Donna DeMille, and dissolved the $328.28 left in the Scholarship Fund to Joanne Cullen and Dar Noesen for their trip to El Salvador. We would now support the Mary's Pence organization, which was beginning to have a life of its own.

— ✿✿✿ —

Energized by the positive outpouring of women in attendance at the 1983 Conference, Women-Church came together on August 16, 1986, to plan for the Second Women-Church Conference which would be held in Cincinnati, October 9–11, 1987.

CHAPTER 20
Using the Media to Confront the Sin of Sexism

In 1985, a group of female filmmakers came to Chicago to shoot part of their film *Behind the Veil: Nuns*. Sue Secker and I were two of the nuns interviewed for the film. Many communities would use the film for their novitiates.

Behind the Veil was "the first film ever to record from a global perspective the turbulent history and remarkable achievements of women in religion, from pre-Christian Celtic communities to the radical sisters of the eighties."[107] The film was directed by Margaret Wescott, written by Gloria Demers, and produced by the National Film Board of Canada. It was filmed in Ireland, Canada, the United States, and Italy. It showed active nuns living and working in Chicago, a Trappist Monastery near Rome, and the exceptional periods in history when women wielded power in religious life. A flyer for the film touts its "exploring the strong female influence in pre-Christian Celtic religions, and the great Abbesses of the Middle Ages [such] as Brigid, Bishop of Kildare and founder of a powerful Christian community in Ireland," and adds, "This was an example of the beneficial potential of women's spirituality." The flyer continues:

Throughout the remainder of the Middle Ages, religious women exuded confidence, performing liturgical rites and

---

107 National Film Board of Canada, Studio D, Flyer for *Behind the Veil*.

founding monasteries all over Europe that were centers of scholarship, medicine, and the arts. The paintings, inventions, tapestries, books, and manuscripts that survive them are eloquent testimony to the achievements.

These achievements were soon dismissed, however, with the revival of misogynistic theories by such eminent and otherwise learned male philosophers as Thomas Aquinas. Their teachings, based on arguments originally put forward by Aristotle, contended that females were deformities, unsuitable to perform priestly functions, certainly not worth educating.

On the basis of these notions, women were excluded from universities for the next eight centuries, and the power and position that religious women once held has not yet been regained. Now women are openly questioning the Church's male hierarchy and seeking some measure of influence in Church decisions. In this film, some of today's active nuns speak about their convictions and the need to re-define the Church to combine spirituality with global politics.[108]

One of my quotes was used on this flyer, *"The Church is in a sinful state as long as it is sexist."—Donna Quinn, O.P.*[109]

— ✿✿✿ —

In the November 21, 1986, issue of *The Chicago Catholic*, Cardinal Bernardin's weekly message was titled "Sexism is the En-

---

108 Ibid.
109 Ibid.

emy!" It was a plea for women to be careful when out alone at night and a look at the statistics on rape and incest. However, he was quick to point out that men are not the enemy—sexism is. He did talk about the sexual responsibility of boys and young men, but he completely ignored sexism in the Church, except for liturgical language. It was as if he was finally able to repeat some statistics and things we had spoken about. It was not enough, but it was a start.[110]

—❀❀❀—

Prior to the second Women-Church Conference, *The Color Purple,* based on the book by Alice Walker, was a popular movie that brought gender issues to the big screen and divided men and women on their opinions about sexism. Some men just did not get it. They seemed to have missed the point of the movie. The point was not how black men are inaccurately portrayed; the point was the entrenched sexism wherein women have for centuries been treated as less than equal—slave to master. Half of the population used and abused by many of the other half. Patriarchy has been around for a long time and the institutions we support are based on it, whether it be government or Church. A feminist is one (male or female) who works to get rid of sexism wherever it is found. It is found after one scratches away classism, racism, and ageism. Underlying the "isms" is the one most deeply ingrained—sexism. Alice Walker, we salute

---

110 Joseph Bernardin, "Sexism Is the Enemy," *The Chicago Catholic,* 21 November, 1986.

you for striking at the heart of this evil![111]

In the seventies, divisions were experienced between those who were nuns and those who were not nuns and between those who were lesbian and those who were not. Now in the eighties, *feminist* and *womanist* were words dividing women along cultural backgrounds. By the time we reached Albuquerque, NM, in 1993 for the third Women-Church Conference, it would be the young women in tension with the older women. But in the end there will always be our sisterhood and that, I think, is something no one will be able to diminish or deny us.

The second Women-Church Conference, "Women-Church: Claiming Our Power," held October 9–11, 1987, encouraged us to claim our economic, political, sexual, and spiritual power by analysis and strategy. We celebrated our strength in symbol and prayer, song and story. We were encouraged to build a base for the empowerment of *women as Church*. Diann Neu coordinated this conference. It was a great success with over 3,000 in attendance and with speakers such as Silvia Cancio, Theresa Kane, and Gloria Steinem.

On October 24, 1987, about 120 people gathered at the University of Illinois at Chicago Newman Center to hear a recap from those who had participated at the conference. Dolores Brooks presented an overview of the event, concluding with a plea to resist the patriarchal "colonization of the mind" that had produced an unjust world order. Rosemary Radford Ruether, Peggy Montes, and Judy Vaughan each analyzed a specific dimension of the

---

111 Chicago Catholic Women, *UPDATE*, Winter 1986.

conference—namely, Power, Racism, and the Future.

With gracious wisdom, Peggy Montes addressed a glaringly pale audience and challenged us to reflect more color among our membership and more empathy in our attitudes.

A panel composed of Anne Carr, Dennis Geaney, and Rosemary Radford Ruether reflected on the Women-Church Movement and its implications. Anne Carr noted that women were leaving the Church in droves and wondered what that will mean to the next generation of children. After speaking to the painful last gasps of a dying clerical culture, Dennis Geaney concluded that "we are never going to move forward unless we can let go." Rosemary Radford Ruether proposed that we are moving toward a "human church" liberated from patriarchy but cautioned against the "false purity" that suggests if we just wipe the institutional church dust from our feet we will be rendered blemish-free.

Judy Vaughan offered this reweaving of the web: that decisions are made every day affecting who will eat, who will starve, who will live, and who will die, and that we must make a commitment not to do unto others as it's been done to us but to work toward the establishment of a new social order—one of compassion and justice.

CHAPTER 21

The Church's Continuing Effort to Make Women Disappear

The first Chicago Call to Action Conference was held October 7, 1978, to further the justice recommendations of the National Conference held by the U.S. bishops in 1976. The Chicago Call to Action had gone from five people—Dan Daley, Jim Duignan, Joan Krebs, Joe O'Brien, and I, meeting regularly—to an alliance of 10 organizations. These 10 organizations played important roles in the founding and development of Call to Action. At its tenth anniversary celebration held November 7, 1987, awards were given by Call to Action to Alliance of Catholic Laity, Association of Chicago Priests, Association for Rights of Catholics in the Church, Chicago Association of Catholic School Teachers, Chicago Catholic Women, Dignity/Chicago, 8th Day Center for Justice, Friendship House, Leadership Conference of Women Religious, and National Assembly of Women Religious.

— ❀❀❀ —

In 1987, the Synod on the Laity in Rome called for a study and action on female deacons, acolytes, and lectors. Recommendations related to all three roles for women had been deleted from the final propositions of the National Call to Action Meeting in 1976. In their place was Proposition 18, asking Pope John Paul II to re-evaluate a 1972 papal decree allowing *laymen* [emphasis added] to be installed in the ministries of acolyte and lector.

The Chicago Catholic reported: "For traditionalists the disappearance of the three proposals was a victory. As one close observer of the process concluded, 'We beat the feminists.' But even if the final propositions concerning women did not go significantly beyond the initial working document, the sight of 15 percent of the delegates from around the world speaking about women, society, and the Church is proof that the subject will remain on the Church's agenda. Irish Cardinal Tomas O'Fiaich said the subject is no longer an 'American aberration.'"[112]

Chicago Catholic Women had an overwhelming response to two questions it put forth to our membership regarding this Synod on the Laity. The first question was, "Do you think that women are making unique contributions to the Church in our time?" This was answered with a resounding "Yes" and examples were given. The second question was, "Do you think women need affirmation from the institutional Church?" Here, however, the answers were mixed.

—❀❀❀—

At the annual meeting of the National Conference of Catholic Bishops in 1987, Cardinal Bernardin, as Chairperson of the NCCB Pro-Life Committee, stated that "the answer to the

112 *The Chicago Catholic*, 6 November 1987.

teen pregnancy problem is not 'quick fix' solutions such as school clinics that promote birth control." The bishops wholeheartedly agreed and unanimously approved a statement drafted by the Pro-Life Activities Committee of the National Conference of Catholic Bishops which rejected the use of such school-based clinics and labeled them "an invitation to social and moral disaster."

The Illinois legislature had recently voted to ban school clinics that dispensed or prescribed contraceptives. The bill had been advocated by the Illinois Catholic Conference, which included the state's bishops and other anti-choice groups around the state. Governor James Thompson vetoed the bill after stating that school-based clinics, even those dispensing condoms and birth control pills, should be regulated by local school officials and not the state.[113]

—❀❀❀—

From June 24 to June 27, 1988, in Collegeville, MN, the bishops met to discuss the 164-page pastoral titled, *Partners in the Mystery of Redemption,* which was to be a pastoral response to women's concerns for Church and society. This letter was headed by Bishop Joseph Imesch and took five years to produce. After revisions it was expected to be put to a vote of U.S. bishops in November 1989. In it they "[labeled] sexism a sin, recommended removing sexist language from the liturgy, banned

---

113 *The Chicago Catholic,* 20 November 1987.

ordination of women, and [banned] artificial birth control."[114]

The third draft said "we [the bishops] encourage women in particular to use their gifts and talents at every level of Church and society." By 1992 this letter was titled "Called to Be One in Christ Jesus." This endeavor began in 1983 and continued into the nineties! Catholic feminists from all over the country urged them not to write it. Feminists preferred that the bishops address sexism in the Church's hierarchy.

Rather than heed this advice, the bishops continued their discussion of women through the pastoral letter while gathered for their spring meeting at the University of Notre Dame, June 18–21, 1992. Again no woman had a voice at these meetings. Women protested this meeting with signs that read: "Every Liturgy that Excludes Women Is Unjust" and "We Want a Church for Our Daughters." Then we celebrated Eucharist.

In 1992, I was quoted in the *Chicago Tribune*: "In the pastoral draft, the bishops denounced sexism, saying that 'both women and men are made in God's image...Therefore, with the whole church, we repeat and affirm the truth that women and men are equal before God and one another...In the spirit of the Second Vatican Council, we denounce sexism as a moral and social evil. Whenever or wherever it is knowingly expressed and acted upon, it is sinful.' The bishops go on to refer to a 1976 proclamation by Pope Paul VI, which stated that women did not resemble Jesus physically and so could not be ordained, in affirming 'an unbroken tradition in the Catholic churches of the East and West of calling only men to ordained priesthood.' This negates

---

114 *The Denver Post*, 12 April 1988.

all previous statements they made condemning sexism."[115]

—❀❀❀—

The Pope made a second visit to the U.S. during September 1987. We encouraged women's organizations to celebrate Liturgies during that weekend of September 18 and 19, with any monies collected to be given to women's projects. Our celebrating was to stand in contrast to the millions of dollars for security and pomp needed for the Pope's trip to the U.S.

---

115 Donna Quinn, "WomenNews: Her Say," *Chicago Tribune*, 31 May 1992.

CHAPTER 22
The Blue House: CCW Creates a Women's Center

CCW was always working at the forefront of social change and tried to respond immediately to issues as they emerged.

Chicago Catholic Women was asked by Barbara Blaine, one of its members, to begin a support group for women who had been sexually abused by priests. Those interested were invited to a meeting on June 4, 1987. This group met twice and then spun off on its own, eventually becoming SNAP (Survivors Network of those Abused by Priests).

On October 10, 1987, there was a Gay and Lesbian March in Washington, D.C., and Chicago Catholic Women was represented by Carol Goodwin and Carol Zientek. On Tuesday, a non-violent protest at the Supreme Court proved to be a rousing finale for the Washington events. Outraged by the Supreme Court's refusal to extend full civil rights to gay and lesbian citizens in one judicial decision after another, over 800 people, including CCW's friend Rick Garcia, were arrested during this civil disobedience action.[116]

— ❈❈❈ —

We moved the annual holiday fundraiser luncheon in 1987

116 *Chicago Catholic Woman-Gram*, January 1988.

to Ann Sather's Restaurant at 929 W. Belmont Ave. on the North Side. At the luncheon, we announced that Genanne Meehan received the 1987 "Woman of the Year" award. We reported that for the new year of 1988, Gerry Gorman would take over as editor of the newsletter with Terry Barnett on legislative info/layout, and Karen Sendziak on activities/current events/photos.

Then came the big announcement—Chicago Catholic Women was moving from its office space at 1307 S. Wabash Ave. to the North Side—to the Blue House as we called it, at 5249 N. Kenmore Ave. In the early days, we were located at the place where I had lived—St. Thomas the Apostle Convent. That was 1974 and 1975. In September 1975, we had office space given to us by 8th Day at 22 E. Van Buren St. and we stayed there until 1979. From August 1979 until January 1988, we worked from 1307 S. Wabash Ave. Now it was time for another move.

During May and June 1986, I had worked with Gretchen Leppke, a Lutheran woman, and many other women from different faith traditions, on an Interfaith Women's Conference that was held June 19–22, 1986, in Chicago. After a year, Gretchen wanted to find an office or place where she could establish a space for people of different faith traditions. She asked if Chicago Catholic Women would be interested—we were— and she found a house owned by the United Methodist Church.

Officially, this house was known as the Susannah Wesley House. It was named after the mother of the founder of the Methodist Church, John Wesley. There is a story that was told that Susannah would pray in her kitchen. This annoyed her husband and her son who preached and led the prayers in the church. Both her husband and her son told her to come to church to hear them preach. She refused, saying that her kitchen was just right for her prayers and her circle of women followers. If she put her apron on the kitchen table, they knew better than to disturb her. She was a strong woman and now Chicago Catholic Women would have a center for strong women named after her.

I remember thinking how wonderful it was to have windows, a kitchen, and large rooms for liturgies and educational programs downstairs, rooms for Chicago Catholic Women offices upstairs, a counseling center, and a resource room for the Women of Faith organization. It would make a perfect Women's Center—a beautiful old house with turn-of-the-century grandeur. We moved into the house in January and had an Open House on Sunday, March 6, 1988, for all members and friends to come and help us celebrate the new beginning.

The afternoon began with a house blessing using Native American imagery, calling forth a blessing on each of the four corners of the Center. The Rev. Kermit Kreuger, pastor of the Epworth United Methodist Church, offered a warm welcome. Representatives of the other organizations housed there introduced themselves and described their work. At this time they were Catholic Advocates for Gay and Lesbian Rights, ChildServe, INFACT, and Women Organized for Reproductive Choice/Chicago Women's AIDS Project. As the years passed, one organization remained—the Chicago Women's AIDS Project—with Cathy Christeller as director. We were happy to have such a needed project under our roof, and Chicago Catholic Women helped them out with clothing and food donations whenever we could.

—❀❀❀—

As we became established in our Blue House, we began to set up programs there. We began to celebrate Eucharist twice a month on the first and third Saturdays, followed by pot luck meals served at the "Coffee House." On the third Saturday, we would also celebrate an Artist-of-the-Month. A woman would bring in a poem she wrote, a picture she painted, photos she took, wood she carved, and she would tell us about her art. We celebrated the artist in every woman.

Because we had the room at the Center and there was an acknowledged need, we began a Counseling Program that offered counseling by able and qualified professionals. This was done by appointment and took place in a small room in the back of the house that afforded privacy.

We even began "Baptisms." Sophia was the first. She was a beautiful baby. We passed her around the circle, each holding her, symbolizing her being part of our Circle of Believers. Joseph was the second baby baptized, a few months later. We enjoyed a party after the naming ceremony. The parents were filled with joy and so were we.

I always thought it would be good to visualize what we were doing at the Women's Center. I drew a rooted base from which would grow a flowering plant. The rooted base was our networking—with Women-Church Convergence, Religious Coalition for Reproductive Choice, Labor Coalition, and our

Drop-In Center for local women and men and those who were visiting from out of town. From this base of members and those who would be interested in Chicago Catholic Women emerged six buds that we truly hoped would continue to blossom. These buds were:

- Art—with our Artist-of-the-Month program
- Liturgy—with our twice-a-month Eucharistic celebrations and retreats
- Education—with our Lenten Series, speakers, and analysis of issues
- Advocacy—working with others on the issues of choice and reproductive rights, lesbian and gay rights, and ordination for women
- Direct Service—working with women at the shelter through our Job-Training Program and employment efforts
- Fundraising—working on our Christmas Benefit Luncheon

Our programs were in full bloom, flourishing, and we reported on them, while always welcoming the involvement of our membership through our monthly newsletters.

—❀❀❀—

Chicago Catholic Women offered its first Retreat for Advent, December 9-11, 1977, at the Fullerton Cenacle with Anne

Metzler, Rosalie Muschal-Reinhardt, and Georgene Wilson. For Lent in 1978, Dolores Brooks directed a day of reflection for women. Retreats and evenings of reflection were always a part of Chicago Catholic Women's work.

We continued our retreats in the fall of every year. We held them at Tower Hill in Sawyer, Michigan, which was on the shores of Lake Michigan and owned by the United Church of Christ. Everyone looked forward to getting away for the weekend to walk, talk, sleep, sing, and laugh. At night, we roasted marshmallows and enjoyed simple meals and taffy apples during the day. The various facilitators we had every year left with an excellent rating by all.

—❀❀❀—

During 1988, Chicago Catholic Women worked to change the policy of the 43 Catholic high schools in Chicago regarding enrolled young women who were not allowed to graduate with their classmates because they were pregnant. One such young woman, Carla, wished to graduate with her class at Unity High School. No amount of telephone calls or pleas from Chicago Catholic Women could make this happen. I received several calls from the faculty asking us to back off. We were not welcome. Chicago Catholic Women knew that this was unfair treatment of females. High school males who became fathers were allowed to stay in school and graduate with their classmates. The Church's sexist policies condemned abortion, birth control, and now pregnant girls in Catholic high schools.

We wrote to Cardinal Bernardin on May 19 about the plight of Carla, a senior. The policy was that the student was to inform the school of her pregnancy and, upon reaching her sixth month, leave the school. Carla notified officials in January that she had just become pregnant but thought she would fall within the six-month deadline and still be able to graduate in May with the rest of her class. She was notified on March 31 that she could not attend her senior prom nor her graduation on June 1. The school was scheduled to close for good at the end of May, putting Carla in its last graduating class. So while policy change was moot for that one school, we wanted policies to change for the other schools whose existence continued.

Carla had her baby girl that summer. Chicago Catholic Women had a shower for her at our Women's Center and took pictures of four generations of women of her family—the baby, Carla, her mother, and grandmother. We had gifts for the new baby and continued our work in the Generations coalition CCW had founded to assist young women with pregnancies.

—❀❀❀—

CCW always had a "Thank You" gathering in June for the board and membership to evaluate the programs of the past year and to plan ahead for the next September through May. In the fall of 1988, Jeannine Gramick spoke about the book she had recently edited called *The Vatican and Homosexuality*. Peggy Thompson from Syracuse University led our discussion on the U.S. bishops' *Pastoral on Women: Partners in the Mystery of*

Redemption. That same year on Saturday, December 10, 1988, Carol Marin, anchor person for CBS News, was our guest speaker at the Annual Benefit Luncheon, speaking on "Ethics in the Media." Awards were given to Monica Cahill, Anne Mayer, and Therese O'Sullivan.

— ❀❀❀ —

We were not without the counter-demonstrators, whether they were painting "Nuns Are Murderers" on the sidewalk because of our stand on choice or whether they showed up at our Mother's Day celebration shouting, "There will never be women priests." But we always did have great media coverage! The Chicago and national newspapers and TV came to do interviews or talk with our members. This just didn't happen automatically. As I did from the beginning of CCW, I spent a great deal of time at the Blue House talking with and faxing the media (at some point it became emailing), and doing follow-up calls both for Chicago Catholic Women and Women-Church Convergence.

— ❀❀❀ —

So many women made the programs at the Center happen. Joanne Cullen, Dar Noesen, Zabrina Decker, Carol Goodwin, Carol Zientek, Chris Pasinski, Nancy Smiegowski, Diane Vanderlinde, Kate Philben, Kathy Giese, Helen Maddix, Nancy Golbeck, Maura Henderson, Karen Allen, Therese Lynch,

Paula Phipps, and Teresa Stiel all helped to create a warm atmosphere at our Coffee House after Liturgies on Saturday nights. They signed up for pot luck dinners and we enjoyed each other's company talking and laughing at small tables and chairs.

Judy Ludwig helped us with secretarial work at the Center, and then Angie Weiss worked with us for four years. Paula Hirschboeck, Sue Secker, and Marie Walter Flood were guest homilists at the Liturgies. We joined with 8th Day Center, National Coalition of American Nuns, National Assembly of Women Religious, Call to Action, and BVM Women's Network for an Ash Wednesday blessing and distributing our own ashes outside of Holy Name Cathedral from 7 to 8 a.m., noon to 1 p.m., and 5 to 6 p.m. Our Lenten Series that year looked at the Feminist images of God—Sophia and Christa.

Our Seder meals were excellent. We celebrated them on the Saturday closest to Passover. No one could improve on the delicious lamb meals that Dar Noesen prepared those years. I bought the candles and decorations, and Joanne Cullen made sure we had the proper prayer service "ingredients," such as apples, parsley, salt water, etc. Dar cooked the best of Seder meals, ending them with three or four decorated lamb cakes. We had four tables set, extending the length of two rooms with seating on both sides for women, men, and children. Dar was also known for her meals cooked for the Coffee House. She and Joanne would arrive in their van and carry in a complete dinner, forgetting nothing. We were always delighted to see the van arrive, knowing it carried the "best cook in Chicago."

One exciting evening in October 1994, Mike Wallace from

60 Minutes came with his whole camera crew to do a program about women celebrating liturgies. He kept asking us if we were subversives but we kept saying, "No," because we definitely were doing this right in the open. I think he meant to ask if we would be viewed as heretics by the Vatican.

So many wonderful years were spent, six and a half in all, at our Women's Center—the Blue House—the Susannah Wesley House. It had many names and so many wonderful people passed through the front door.

CHAPTER 23

Mother's Day Protests and CCW's Call for a Catholic Church Boycott Until Women Are Ordained

Chicago Catholic Women called for a national boycott of Catholic churches on Mother's Day 1988. It was a way of saying, "We will no longer silently tolerate from our Church what we would vocally protest from our governments...We cannot look for moral leadership to a Church entrenched in sexual hypocrisy. When we presume to coin phrases like 'seamless garment,' [referring to the "consistent pro-life" ethic promoted Cardinal Bernardin] we had better be sure our fabric is made of strong moral fiber and interweaves us all, in equality and honesty."[117]

So, on Sunday May 8, 1988, we kicked off the boycott with a demonstration at Holy Name Cathedral downtown from 9:30 to 10:30 a.m., followed by an alternative liturgy at our Women's Center at 5249 N. Kenmore Ave. at 11 a.m. We asked women to withdraw support from their local church for this day: no Mass attendance, no choir singing, no bread baking. Instead we invited families and friends to join us, "for a morning of celebration and hope for the future."[118]

We were asked why we chose Mother's Day. It seemed most appropriate for pointing out how the Church continued to squander the gifts of its women. This is a day on which the

117 Chicago Catholic Women, *UPDATE*, May 1988.
118 Ibid.

institutional Church, with great fanfare, applause, and flowers, "honors" women, allowing us our annual ascent to the pulpit. "We maintain that we reject this tokenism. We will forego the one-day testimonial to our virtue in favor of our own commemoration of our gifts, pain, struggles. We want justice, not daisies."[119] The boycott was endorsed by 38 groups across the U.S.—from California east to Boston and Washington, D.C., and from Texas north to Minneapolis and Cincinnati—and the Netherlands.

This Mother's Day protest and boycott would continue through 1994, and ultimately expand in scope.

We had blue ribbons printed with the words "Ordain Women Now." We sent those out to feminists with the following, "We hope that this will hasten the day when the Catholic Church can get back to the reason for being; namely, to be a 'discipleship of equals,' a Eucharistic community which is a justice community."

Some women wrote in that they long ago gave up on caring what the Pope and priests do. They could no longer identify with the political structure of the Church and ended with, *Why do you?* Others asked us to include in the boycott school workers, parish workers, hospital workers, rectory workers, and all others doing church-affiliated work—even for a day.

Thereafter on Mother's Day for several years, we invited speakers from different women's groups in Chicago to speak out on women's issues. In our call to open the Church to women we called for ordination of women, equal representation in

---

119 Ibid.

the College of Cardinals, equal representation in the National Conference of Catholic Bishops, and the use of inclusive language in all churches.

We were often told to leave the steps of the Cathedral by the ushers of the parish. There was always that tension between it being a "parish church" and something more symbolic—the Cathedral of the Archdiocese, everyone's Church. Our presence on the steps of Holy Name was emblematic of our not being welcomed or treated as equals inside the church. We marched with large signs and we always leafleted the people going into or coming out of the church. Our leaflet contained the following statistics:

- There are 864,379,000 Catholics in the world
- There are 54,918,989 Catholics in the U.S.
- 55% of the above are women
- The Church has 0 (ZERO) women in its governing (DECISION-MAKING) body.

All laws, rules, and policies about <u>WOMEN</u> are made by the following men:

	NUMBER OF MEN	NUMBER OF WOMEN
Pope	1 Male	0
Cardinals in the World	151 Males	0
Cardinals in the U.S.	9 Males	0
Bishops in the World	3,138 Males	0
Bishops in the U.S.	352 males	0

We then invited all to join us as we celebrated Eucharist on our own on the steps of Holy Name Cathedral, often with close to 150 people, in honor of all those women who had gone before us and our daughters who would be here after us. We brought the breads. We brought the candles. We brought the musical instruments and songs. We invited the speakers. Everyone was welcome.

For two years, after our celebration at Holy Name Cathedral, we walked three blocks to the Jewish Temple Kol Ami for breakfast, which CCW members brought and set up for everyone. We were very grateful to the people of Kol Ami and to Rabbi Kaiman, who graciously took us in and let us use their gathering room for further conversation and breakfast.

One year we took out an ad in the *National Catholic Reporter*, asking bishops to stop all ordinations until women were included, and that all people join in a boycott of liturgies until women were ordained.

The following organizations from around the city joined us on May 13, 1990, for our Mother's Day witness: National Coalition of American Nuns, Mujeres Latinas En Accion, Catholic Advocates for Lesbian & Gay Rights, Loyola Women's Center, National Organization for Women–Chicago, Illinois NOW, Religious Coalition for Reproductive Choice, Dignity/Chicago, Women of Faith Resource Center, Planned Parenthood Emergency Clinic, Defense Coalition Women for Peace, University of Chicago Women's Union, and Guatemala En Lucha. We called that year for the ordination of women, equal representation in the College of Cardinals, and use of inclusive language in all churches. Once again, we called everyone to invite their mothers to join us outside of Holy Name Cathedral from 10 a.m. to Noon.

Music has always inspired and been an important part of the Women's Movement and CCW. We listened to and sang along with Cris Williamson, Kristin Lems, Marsie Silvestro, Carolyn McDade, Colleen Fulmer, and Kathy Sherman. At our Mother's Day Witness/Protest on May 5, 1992, we sang "A Rock Will Wear Away," with music by Meg Christian and words by Holly Near.[120] We also stated that we were outraged by the absence of women in the leadership of the Catholic Church and by the decisions made about women by these men. Women must be given the right to vote in the Church!

One year three male parishioners of Holy Name Cathedral screamed and waved fists and a cane at us as they walked out of the church. We continued our songs and continued to pass out our Women-Church buttons to participants. We were creating the new, while boycotting the patriarchy."[121]

By May 1994, Chicago Catholic Women was calling on all Catholics to "Stop everything" in the Catholic Church until women are ordained.

Our campaign was threefold:

1. That all bishops stop ordaining men until women are also included in those considered for ordained ministry.

---

120 Meg Christian (music), Holly Near (words), "The Rock Will Wear Away."
121 *National Catholic Reporter*, 22 October 1993.

2. That all Catholics take the prophetic, and for some, difficult step of boycotting all Eucharistic Liturgies until women are ordained.

3. That in those instances where boycotting is not feasible, that all who attend Eucharistic Liturgies wear blue armbands or blue Ordain Women Now lapel ribbons to signal their affirmation of the ordination of women.

We sent a blue lapel ribbon to Cardinal Bernardin asking him to wear it to signify his support for ordaining women. 105 women and men and 18 organizations signed on to support this effort.

Chicago Catholic Women also urged ordained priests in the Archdiocese to stop celebrating Eucharistic liturgies until women's ordination is permitted. "The Church wonders why young people are not interested and why funding isn't there. Do they ever wonder why they continue this immoral and unjust practice of including anyone provided that person is male?" asked Joanne Cullen, a CCW Coordinator.[122]

The *Chicago Tribune* reported a response: "An Archdiocesan spokesperson said the chances were 'slim to none' that any priest would actually give up celebrating mass. Donna Quinn, who has been boycotting the Eucharist since Mother's Day over the issue of women's ordination, agreed. That's why Chicago Catholic Women included a second option in its letter to priests,

---

122 Ibid.

asking them to name the sin of sexism during the mass until women are ordained."[123]

By Mother's Day of 1995, we asked all people to renew their endorsement of the boycott and their commitment to women's ordination and full equality in the Church. And, instead of having Mother's Day at Holy Name Cathedral, as we had done for the past seven years, we asked that all have a Circle of Celebration on Mother's Day wherever they may gather to celebrate the gifts of women and to say *No More* to the Church's violence toward young girls and women with its continual reiteration that females are not good enough to receive all the Sacraments.

---

123 *Chicago Tribune*, 14 November 1993.

CHAPTER 24
Working for Justice in the Nineties and Moving to the South Side

We opened a new decade, the nineties, with a new logo. This new logo was perfect as the two C's (Chicago Catholic) formed the W (Women) and were within the feminist symbol. I sketched what I wanted and Mary Rosebraugh came to our rescue by cleaning it up and drawing it perfectly.

I went out to Washington, D.C., on behalf of Chicago Catholic Women, for the March for Women's Equality–Women's Lives, sponsored by the National Organization for Women in 1989, and again in 1992. In 1989, while taking the D.C. metro train, I remember feeling so surprised that so many young men had joined our March for Women. In 1992, Manny Tuteur held the banner for Chicago Catholic Women, and I held the National Coalition of American Nuns banner as we marched for women. Many bystanders cheered for Manny as they saw "Catholic" in the banner she held; and they shouted, "Right on Sister," as I went by holding the banner with "Nuns" on it. There was hope for our cause.

—❈❈❈—

Because so many gay high school students faced possible ridicule, ostracism, and violence from their peers, as well as parental rejection, they had doubts about their own worth and a significantly higher rate of suicide than their heterosexual peers. Chicago Catholic Women worked during the early nineties with Horizon, an organization for gays and lesbians. We sent a letter and questionnaire to the principals and counselors of all the Catholic high schools in the Chicago area. We heard from about 26 high schools. Horizons had prepared a packet for the public schools in Chicago and so we prepared packets for the Catholic high schools in Chicago that responded to the questionnaire. Several schools thanked us and said they would be more aware of the needs of gay and lesbian students.

—❈❈❈—

Chicago Catholic Women sponsored a one-day conference, "Beyond Dissent: Decisions for Women-Church," held on Saturday, October 13, 1990, at the Congress Hotel, 520 S. Michigan Ave., in Chicago. Conference speakers explored issues of dissent facing the Catholic Church in light of the recent Vatican's document on dissent. Speakers included Rosemary Radford Ruether from Garrett-Evangelical Theological Seminary and Eugene Bianchi, Professor of Theology at Emory University. They were writing a book, *A Democratic Catholic Church: The Reconstruction of Roman Catholicism*, which was published in 1992. Mary Jean Collins from Catholics for a Free Choice, Silvia Cancio from Greater Cincinnati Women-Church, Margaret Traxler from Institute of Women Today, and Leslie Brown from Women in

Prisons Around the World spoke in the afternoon. Around 250 participants shared their concerns for the new decade.

—❀❀❀—

The Peoria National Organization for Women invited me to speak at their meeting in Peoria, IL, on Monday, November 5, 1990, at the Unitarian Universalist Church. The meeting was to explore the issues of reproductive choice: what it means to us personally and to all women; why and how we make the choices we make; and why we, as women, must be free to make them. I was asked as the director of Chicago Catholic Women to facilitate a discussion by women, sharing their fears, concerns, and situations around this topic. A notice went out to all members and to the media that this would be a safe space and any behavior that is threatening would not be tolerated.

John J. Myers, Bishop of Peoria, had written a pastoral message on abortion in June. In that written message, Myers encouraged "pro-choice Catholics to consider abstaining from Holy Communion," and he wrote that there is "no such thing as an authentic pro-choice Catholic."[124]

On Monday, October 22, 1990, Bishop Myers called Kaye Ashe, President of the Sinsinawa Dominicans, asking that she forbid me to speak in Peoria, or he would write to Rome. She responded that she did not order our women as to what to do and advised him to call me directly. He called me that after-

---

124 Dean Olsen, "Pro-Choice Nun Defies Peoria Bishop," *Journal Star Peoria*, 1 November 1990: A4.

noon, but I was on the telephone with a probation officer, regarding a woman doing community service for us, so I told him that I would get back to him.

When I called him, he told me not to go to Peoria. I asked him, "Do all the women in Peoria have his position on this issue?"

"No," he said, but he had sent a survey out about women's issues.

"Did you include abortion?"

"No."

I told him to sit down with Peoria NOW women. (Shelly Schnupp-Daily, President of the Peoria Chapter of NOW told me later that they had asked for this and had invited him to the meeting but he declined.) I told him that he must bring peace and not be involved in a knock-down, drag-out fight with the women in his diocese. I asked for his phone number to try to bring him and NOW together. Then I asked him how old he was. When he replied, "49," I almost fell off my chair. I said in amazement that he was younger than I was (53) and I couldn't believe someone so young could be a bishop with such conservative ideas.

Bishop Myers followed up our telephone conversation with a letter to me stating "...I wish to reaffirm my formal request that you not participate in this or any other pro-choice event within the Diocese of Peoria. For you or any person in consecrated life to do so would be, in my judgment, extremely inappropriate pastorally. I ask that you not attend any such meetings."[125]

---

125 Bishop John Myers, Peoria, Letter to Donna Quinn, 22 October 1990.

My first thought was *how feudal!*—the bishop of the fiefdom, the lord of the manor, drawing a circle around the land he "owned" and forbidding entrance as he desired. If he could tell me that I couldn't travel to Peoria because it was his diocese, then any bishop anywhere could tell any woman that she could not enter a particular city because it was his diocese. In essence, he was denying freedom of travel, assembly and speech, rights I believe our country is founded upon. I thought of my Grandmother Quinn, who risked and lost her life on the boat from Limerick, Ireland, to this land of the "free," travelling with my grandfather and three children, the youngest of whom was my dad. No, in the name of my Irish grandmother, this bishop was not going to prevent a Chicago Catholic Woman from traveling to Peoria.

I asked Margaret Traxler to come with me. She said, "Yes," and brought another nun, Bernie Galvin, with her. With the media reporting on this event, it tripled the numbers expected for the evening. People were sitting on radiators and on the floor and all were eager to express their feelings about the issue.

Sure enough, Bishop Myers wrote to Rome about me and a letter was written back to the President of the Sinsinawa Dominicans. My file in Rome continued to grow.

—❁❁❁—

On Saturday, May 11, 1991, we had a fun night of signature and song at the Women's Center with Mary Hunt speaking and autographing her new book, *Fierce Tenderness: A Feminist Theology of Friends*. She was marvelous and drew a large crowd.

People were sitting in two rooms and in the hallways.

We also had a drawing for a custom crochet afghan, made by Angie Weiss. The donations went to our Job-Training Program at the shelter. With the donations, we were able to help five women in the program. Margaret Traxler's name was drawn and she decided on the size, color, and design of the afghan. Angie had the beautiful afghan ready to present to Margaret at our Christmas Fundraiser Luncheon that year.

— ❀❀❀ —

Chicago Catholic Women Coordinators for the 1992–1993 year were Karen Allen, Joanne Cullen, Pat Eggert, Anna Marie Franko, Nancy Golbeck, Mary Hill, Judy Ludwig, Therese Lynch, Darlene Noesen, Carol Zientek, and myself.

— ❀❀❀ —

The Pope released his encyclical on October 5, 1993. Called *Veritatis Splendor* (The Splendor of Truth), it was 183 pages and six years in the writing. The Pope did not invoke the ultimate authoritative language of papal infallibility. He stated that the flock, often led by theologians who debate Church teachings, is drifting away from acknowledging absolute objective morality, which he called "universal and unchanging moral norms" on the one hand and recognized "intrinsically evil acts" on the other. The encyclical warned that the Church faces a "genuine crisis" of "overall and systematic calling into question of traditional moral doctrine." For conservatives, the Pope's letter was viewed as necessary and successful; for liberals, it was seen as a futile attack on growing disobedience to church teachings.[126]

Meanwhile, Reuters reported that "the British House of Commons voted to back the ordination of women priests in the Church of England. The move by the mother church of the world's 70 million Anglicans is its most crucial since splitting with Rome in 1534, dashing any hopes of swift progress on reunification talks with the Roman Catholic Church. On Saturday, March 12, 1994, 32 Anglican women were ordained by the Bishop of Bristol. The Vatican spokesperson, Joaquin Navarro-Valls, said Pope John Paul II 'had clearly and publicly affirmed that the ordination of women also constitutes a profound obstacle to every hope of reunion between the Catholic Church and the Anglican Communion.'"[127]

—❀❀❀—

In 1993, the Women's Hall of Fame inducted 35 of the country's most prominent women, including Rosa Parks, Georgia O'Keeffe, and Betty Friedan. This was the largest group of inductees in the Hall's 24-year history. In the past, the list included no more than four women because the hall stipulated that only two living and two dead women be inducted per year. The rules ultimately changed because board members felt they were pitting the accomplishments of women and their impor-

---

126 Michael Hirsley, "Papal Encyclical Confronts Crisis of Not Following Church Beliefs," *Chicago Tribune*, 6 October 1993, Section 2:2.
127 *Chicago Tribune*, 23 March 1994, Section 1:3.

tance in history against each other, and that would contradict the organization's ideology. Susan Butler, the Hall of Fame's director, said the ceremony is meant to honor the women and showcase the influence of women in the nation's society. "All of them are risk takers, and all of them have been willing to jump out there and do something that women have not done or have not done well in the past," Butler said.[128]

— ❀❀❀ —

On April 13, 1994, the Vatican announced that it had given its approval for girls to act as altar servers at Roman Catholic Masses but emphasized that the move was not a step toward female priests.[129] At least one-third of the parishes in the Chicago Archdiocese already had female altar servers by this time.[130]

By 2001 a statement by the Vatican said bishops cannot require their priests to use female altar servers. While upholding bishops' authority to permit use of female servers in their dioceses, the Congregation for Divine Worship and the Sacraments said the use of male servers should be especially encouraged, in part because altar boys are a potential source of priestly vocations. "Such an authorization may not, in any way, exclude men or, in particular, boys from the service of the altar, nor require that priests of the diocese would make use of female servers," the Congregation said, "...Indeed, the obligation to support groups of altar boys will always remain, not least of

128 Associated Press, *The Denver Post*, 15A, 1993.
129 Tribune Wires, *Chicago Tribune*, 14 April 1994.
130 *The New World*, 15 April 1994.

all due to the well-known assistance that such programs have provided since time immemorial in encouraging future priestly vocations." In addition, it said, "it is perhaps helpful to recall that the non-ordained faithful do not have a right to service at the altar, but are given their mandate by church pastors."[131]

—❀❀❀—

As the Archdiocese of Chicago prepared for its yearlong sesquicentennial celebration in 1993, Cardinal Bernardin, who had celebrated 10 years in Chicago the year before, was now faced with allegations of sexual abuse by a former pre-seminary student.[132] Bernardin denied these allegations and was later proven innocent, but it took a toll on him as the years passed.

Chicago Catholic Women celebrated its twentieth anniversary in the summer of 1994 with an announcement of a move from the center on Kenmore to a storefront on 95th Street in Evergreen Park. We had a great center at the Susannah Wesley House for six and a half years. Now it was time to have a storefront with off-the-street access, with windows to showcase and sell the items made by the women in our Job-Training Program. Chicago Catholic Women had been in two locations downtown and then in Uptown on the North Side. Now we would be on the South Side of Chicago.

I had moved south two years before this, so the ride to our

---

131 *National Catholic Reporter*, 11 January 2002, reporting on a July 27, 2001, letter responding to a query from an unidentified bishop that was published in December 2001 in *Notitiae*, the bulletin of the Congregation for Divine Worship and the Sacraments.
132 Michael Hirsley, *Chicago Tribune*, 14 November 1993, Sec. 1:19.

Women's Center on the North Side had become a journey for me, especially as I had moved an aunt in with me and took care of her until her death in January 1994.

Chicago Catholic Women began moving into our new location the weekend of August 12–14, 1994. It was a stressful time for me because in July we found out that my sister Joyce had cancer. Bill and I took turns for the next two years going out to Denver while she went through treatments and remission and then more treatments.

Before CCW moved to the South Side in December 1994, I sat down with the leadership of the group at our North Side Center and told them that they were strong enough to keep the programs going at the Center on their own. They did keep the liturgies and retreats going and soon named themselves Chicago Women-Church. They remain a strong, reliable group of women who continue to be an example of change for the generations to follow.

—❀❀❀—

The beginning days in Evergreen Park meant setting up our space and a meeting with the mayor, who liked to meet with every group before they moved into the community. I met with him and explained who we were. Mary Rosebraugh painted our name across the huge windows which brightened the whole storefront. We displayed the baskets, beads, and meditation books made by the members of Chicago Catholic Women and the women in our Job-Training Program. We hosted programs in this bright room that included a Lenten Series, making clay pots, and liturgies for young and old. We continued our work in the Woodlawn area at the shelter and the senior building. Margot Tunney helped in the office for two years and Angie Weiss came back again and helped out for the next four years.

We did not have an annual luncheon at our Women's Center on 95th Street our first year there; but instead had an open house on December 10, 1994.

— ✿✿✿ —

Women went to Beijing in September 1995 for a U.N. Fourth World Conference on Women. Chicago Catholic Women held a liturgy and discussion at our new center on October 7, inviting local women who had gone to Beijing to share their stories with us. On November 4, Susan Scherkenbach, a Marist Sister, shared her 24 years of experience in Peru. The women on the South Side of Chicago were interested in learning about women from other parts of the world.

— ✿✿✿ —

We held our 1995 Christmas Luncheon Fundraiser on December 9 at The Old Barn Restaurant in the southwest suburb of Burbank. The guest speaker was Sheila Lyne, Commissioner of Chicago Deptartment of Public Health, who spoke on health issues for women and children. Awards were given to the Sisters of Mercy, celebrating 150 years serving the people of Chicago

(1846–1996); Margaret Traxler, celebrating 50 years as a School Sister of Notre Dame; and volunteers Anna Marie Franko, Kay Philpott, Mary Lou Sullivan, and Margot Tunney.

—❀❀❀—

Our Lenten Program continued. On March 9, 1996, Mary Lou Sullivan presented her Creative Memories program with an afternoon of how to make great photo albums to preserve the memories of all those wonderful people who have gone before us or the people who presently give us life.

—❀❀❀—

Our Christmas luncheon fundraiser in 1996 was on Saturday, December 14. We invited Kathy O'Malley and Judy Markey, the talk show hosts from WGN Talk Radio. We had music by Kristin Lems; and gave awards made by the residents of Misericordia to the Sinsinawa Dominicans celebrating 150 years serving the people of South America, Central America, Europe, and the U.S. (1847–1997); Jackie Edens, Assistant Commissioner of Family Support Services at the Department of Human Services; Betty V. Holcomb, Co-Chair of the Religious Coalition for Reproductive Choice-Chicago; and Jan Schakowsky, U.S. Representative from the Evanston, Skokie, and Rogers Park in Chicago. The luncheon was filled to capacity with over 400 women attending. We would definitely need a bigger banquet hall for next year.

CHAPTER 25
The Synod on Religious Life

It was announced by the Vatican that a synod would be held in Rome in October 1994 on "The Consecrated Life and its Role in the Church and in the World." Recent synods (meetings of bishops with the Pope to discuss a particular topic) called for a synod on the laity (1987) and a synod on priestly ministry (1991). In the preliminary document (known as *Lineamenta*), the Synod on Religious Life, according to the Secretary General of the Synod Council, Belgian Archbishop Jan Schotte, was "intended to prompt an in-depth reflection on the topic by the pastors of the church and by all other interested parties."[133]

After many letters back and forth with the Synod's organizers, the International Councils of Major Superiors obtained a concession that 20 religious would be allowed to be present (10 women and 10 men would be there as general superiors), however, "they would not be allowed a vote as this was, after all, a Synod of Bishops." Archbishops Bernardin and Quinn were representing the U.S. bishops at this synod.[134]

The National Coalition of American Nuns planned to be in Rome for this Synod on Religious Life. We flew over on October 4, 1994. Members who went were Dee Estes and her

---

133 Peter Hebblethwaite, "Keeping Sisters in Their Place at Synod on Religious," *National Catholic Reporter*, 30 July 1993.
134 Ibid.

14-year old daughter Margie Estes, Peggy Thompson and her mother Irene Thompson, Liz Smyth, Jeannine Gramick, Anne Mary Dooley, Michelle Olley, Margaret Traxler, and myself. NCAN had a three-part strategy. Peggy Thompson and Jeannine Gramick sought and then organized the input from nuns around the world on the questions asked in the preliminary document (*Lineamenta*). Anne Mary Dooley and Michelle Olley organized the forums we held in Rome at various locations on specific topics of the preliminary document. Margaret Traxler and I organized what would be the first protest ever held in St. Peter's Square.

Nuns who were in Rome at this time but whose generalates were from as far away as Ireland or Africa were invited to speak at the NCAN forums we held there. Great conversations were generated by those in attendance. We stayed at the School Sisters of Notre Dame's house in Rome and experienced their tremendous generosity. We dined with them and listened to stories told by their nuns who were stationed all over the world. What a wealth of information and sharing we had with women on this trip.

As we were representing the various magazines or newsletters of our organizations, we obtained press credentials for the Synod. We had been doing this at Bishops' Conferences since the seventies. This gave us access to information and decisions going on at the meetings inside and allowed us to ask questions at the press conferences. Like always, I took every opportunity in Rome to push the establishment on our concerns—about women's role in the Church, women not in leadership roles, women being denied ordination, and about women religious not allowed a voice and vote at this Synod on Religious Life. The bishops at the table on the stage in the auditoriums were forced to respond while the media took notes. Some bishops did include our concerns at the conversations inside, and we heard that some bishops, especially those from economically poorer regions, supported women in leadership roles. We tried using the internet with some success to report our daily happenings back to the States.

It was 1994, and I still found that no matter what part of the world women were from, they all had the same experiences with the Church. Women reported to us that they "were tired of being the spokes on the wheel"; they wanted to be "a part of the hub." They were the workers and faithful educators of the next generations, but received very little in return. They were not respected for their gifts. They were not ordained. They were not allowed to preach the Word.

While we were in Rome, I wanted to meet with Cardinal Bernardin, so I called and set up a meeting for Margaret Traxler and me at his quarters in the North American College in Rome. Margaret needed help walking but we made it to his door for our 3:30 appointment on October 20. Upon opening the door he greeted us and as he led us into his rooms he right away made some comments about our wanting to see him regarding the allegations of sexual abuse made against him. As I wasn't sure what he was referring to, I must have looked puzzled. When it dawned on me, I said that we didn't come for that reason.

The three of us relaxed as he showed us around his apartment.

We sat down and the conversation continued. I asked him if he believed women should be ordained. He answered, "Yes, Donna, I do think women should be ordained, but it won't happen in the lifetime of this Pope." I went away from that visit with a greater spirit of hope in my heart, and a needed vindication of all the work we did, through all those statements and all the years he was president of the NCCB, and later Cardinal of Chicago, when he did not support this issue.

The next day, NCAN became the first organization ever to protest in St. Peter's Square. We marched across the square to protest the institutional Church's Synod on Religious Life taking place without voice or vote by women religious. I had carried to Rome three long signs printed on canvas. A few of us had gone to the square previously and talked about what we might do, but on the morning of our march, none of us knew exactly what was going to happen. Our numbers were small. Michelle Olley and I led the procession carrying the sign that read "The National Coalition of American Nuns." Dee and Margie Estes each took a side of the sign that read "Women Want to Be a Part...Not Apart." Margaret Traxler and Irene Thompson had the third banner: "They Are Meeting About Us...Without Us." Three of the sign carriers were nuns and three were friends of NCAN.

CBS had their *60 Minutes* Paris satellite there to record the episode. As we started marching, a strange feeling of strength came over me. I wanted to lead the group closer to St. Peter's steps, so Michelle and I headed that way, step by step, slowly moving closer. Margaret shouted to go faster, and I asked

Michelle what song we should sing. She suggested "We Shall Overcome." About halfway across St. Peter's Square, the police came up to us and asked us what we were doing. I said that we were protesting the Synod going on inside. People started gathering around and as they heard us they shouted in agreement with us. This agitated the police and they asked for the banners. I did not want to give it to them, but as I rolled it up they grabbed it away from me. Irene was able to put hers down the front of her sweater, so we did salvage the "They Are Meeting About Us—Without Us" sign.

They walked us to the Vatican police station on the right side of the square. A crowd was gathering, and Michelle slipped outside of the Vatican circle and escaped into the crowd. This left five of us detained by the police for about an hour: Irene, Dee, her 14-year old daughter Margie, Margaret, and I. Margaret and I were the only nuns in the group. The police asked me if I was really a nun, dressed the way I was, because they were used to nuns dressed in habits in Rome. They wanted our passports but I didn't want to and I gave them my press credentials instead. It is a good thing we weren't searched. The others gave up their passports. We were grateful for the translator from CBS, Allen Pizzey. After much questioning and going back and forth to their commanders, it was decided that they would let us go. We were happy to be released and also happy that we succeeded in our demonstration for all women while we were in Rome.

—❀❀❀—

I went back to Chicago to continue our work and then to Denver to visit my sister in treatment for cancer. A good friend, Joan Leonard, died in April 1995 of cancer. Bernardin went back to Chicago and by June 1995 it was announced that he had pancreatic cancer. My sister, Joyce, died in July 1996 and Cardinal Bernardin died in November 1996.

When Bernardin came to Chicago in 1982, he said, "I am your brother Joseph." He lived that way during his last years. When he first came to Chicago, he was a professional administrator. When he died he was living like our brother Joseph—a minister to the poor, sick, and dying.

CHAPTER 26
Celebrating 20 Years of Accomplishments of
Chicago Catholic Women

From its founding in 1974, Chicago Catholic Women was off to a spirited start, responding to the need for work on women's rights in Church and society. Looking back over the first 20 years, Chicago Catholic Women had done quite a bit of "birthing" over the years, not only in Chicago but also in other parts of the country helping women found organizations:

In the seventies, we helped birth:

- Women's Ordination Conference, 1975
- Women of the Church Coalition, 1977
- Chicago Call to Action, 1978

In the eighties, we helped birth:

- Women-Church Convergence, 1983
- Boston Women-Church
- Sinsinawa Women's Network
- Greater Cincinnati Women-Church
- Generations (a Chicago-based coalition working with pregnant teens)
- ElderCare (a Chicago program working with seniors in

Woodlawn)
- Job-Training Program for the women at St. Martin de Porres House of Hope
- Mary's Pence

In the nineties, we helped birth:

- Chicago Women-Church

Some of Chicago Catholic Women's accomplishments in our first two decades include:

- Being the first women's group in the U.S. to actively include both nuns and laywomen
- Initiating the Women's Agenda before 1975, and at the National Call to Action in 1976
- Working towards passing the Equal Rights Amendment
- Working to bring organizations together in coalition and convergence
- Holding conferences with other groups on a national level
- Speaking for women's issues in Central America and in Europe
- Supporting efforts to keep reproductive choice safe, legal, accessible, and (hopefully one day) funded
- Supporting Marches for Women's Lives in D.C. and California

- Supporting U.S. marches, meetings, and rallies for women

- Originating the idea of sending up pink smoke to signify that grey smoke and white smoke left women out of papal elections and synods that were called to promulgate policies and practices of the Church

- Working on giving women the right to vote in the Catholic Church

- Holding Eucharistic liturgies on the steps of the Cathedral on Mother's Day

- Holding Eucharistic liturgies downtown, on the North Side, in Hyde Park, in Logan Square, and at colleges and universities every week so that all would be welcome

- Holding conferences on dissent, ordination, sexuality, spirituality, survival, and issues of the day

- Hosting book signings to support women authors

- Reaching out to Protestants, Kol Ami Temple, and joining with organizations working for justice issues in Church and society

- Helping African-American children during the busing crisis in Chicago and working to end other forms of racism

- Working with Catholic high schools regarding policies on young women finding themselves with an unplanned pregnancy

- Working with Catholic high school counselors regarding the suicide rate of lesbian and gay students

- Working with AIDS/HIV coalitions

- Working with unordained preachers in the Archdiocese
- Protesting the ordinations of male-only seminarians
- Working with the Paluch Co. and the NCCB on the use of inclusive language in hymns, songs, and prayers
- Working with women and children in shelters, originating a job-training curriculum, elder care program, entrepreneurship program, and parenting skills program
- Finding open arms from other venues after being refused the use of Catholic facilities by pastors and bishops for our fundraisers or conferences
- Working on a national survey, after Cardinal Bernardin died, to gather the qualities desired in a cardinal and suggest possible women who might fill this role. Seventy-three qualities were listed and sixteen women were named as possible choices for cardinal. These were published, but not realized.
- Rallying to success on behalf of female altar servers. After much discussion and input, the grandmothers won out with their 1983 protest on the steps of the Art Institute in Chicago where the traveling Vatican Art Collection exhibit was on display. Grandmothers said they saw no difference in their granddaughters and grandsons when it came to serving at the altar. By 1994 Bernardin and the Vatican had shifted their position on female altar servers and they were welcomed in that role.

CHAPTER 27
A Woman Cardinal for Chicago

Cardinal Bernardin died in November 1996 and so Chicago Catholic Women, knowing that there was a vacancy to fill, initiated a search in January 1997 for a woman to serve as Cardinal. We stated in a letter to our mailing list, which exceeded 2,000 names at that point, that we were also aware of the failing health of the Pope and his ability to resign his post as Bishop of Rome, just as he had encouraged other bishops to do at age 75. We were looking for women candidates for this position as well. We therefore began a campaign asking participants to nominate a woman they would like to see as Cardinal, state the qualifications they would like to see in a Cardinal, and ask the nominee first, before sending in her name, if she would be willing to serve as Cardinal of Chicago or...as Pope.

We added: "Since at this time in the history of the Church it must be very painful for the College of Cardinals and the Papacy not to include the voice of half of the Church (women), we invite other organizations and individuals to help the Church become inclusive of all its members by joining us in this campaign to include women."

The survey was sent to people across the United States. We wanted to show that the qualities needed to be Cardinal of Chicago certainly reside in the female gender as well as males called to this ministry. Chicago Catholic Women called for a new selection process—one that does not discriminate based on gender. We have become too used to this discrimination! If we left people out of a selection process because of their race, people in Chicago would be outraged, and rightly so. CCW and our likeminded peers and friends knew gender discrimination to be just as immoral. We thought no new Cardinal should be selected until the selection process was changed. Copies of the survey were sent to Rome and to the NCCB.

Over 200 people responded to the survey, listing 73 qualities or traits they would like to see in a cardinal and putting forth the names of 17 women. Results were announced in February 1997. The women named were:

Kaye Ashe	Ann Halloran
Mary Ellen Caron	Jose Hobday
Joan Chittister	Theresa Kane
Patsy Crowley	Andrea Laiacona
Mary DeCock	Donna Quinn
Jean Fecteau	Rosemary Radford Ruether
Anna Marie Franko	Margaret Traxler
Maureen Fiedler	Miriam Therese Winter
Edwina Gateley	

The following are the responses from the Survey on Qualities of Cardinal of Chicago, we presented in February 1997.[135]

---

135 Chicago Catholic Women, Survey on Cardinal of Chicago, February 1997.

Qualities for Cardinal of Chicago

Ability to see the BIG picture: women, justice, religions (not
just Roman Catholic)

Ability to speak and write

Ability to delegate and let go of minutiae

Fearless of institutions

Compassion

Open-mindedness

Respect for individual conscience

Ability to lead with love

Sensitive to all humankind

Willing to spend more time with the poor, sick, homeless

Open to different prayers and liturgical functions

Empathy for and commitment to the economically disadvantaged people in society

Commitment to women in leadership roles

Commitment to the environment

Sense of humor

Vision

Courage

Prayerful

Strong faith

Risk taker

Gentleness

Kindness

Strength

Love and zeal for justice

Open to dialogue
Seeks creative and responsible solutions to problems
Relies on democratic process
Kind, friendly, intelligent woman
Courage to speak out
Peaceful
Pastoral
Healer
Some understanding of human nature
Independent thinker
Listens to diverse viewpoints
Committed to women's equality
Feminist
Persistence
Optimism
Impatience with the patriarchal church
Not afraid to take a stand
Dedication to her God and her church
Sensitivity to diverse expressions of Catholicism
Willingness to risk excommunication
Respecter of persons, religions, and races
Futurist
Incarnate Sophia
Understand how city works
Politically aware
Experience in the public arena
Understands the social/political crisis of city and nation from

perspective of the poor
Facilitator
Administrator
Good Liturgist
A woman who would lead and support the right to have
    women ordained
Sagacity
Wisdom
Ability to disagree publicly if principles are involved
Knowledge of Church history, laws, and teachings of Jesus
Ability to see changes and directions the Church needs to
    go—not antiquated
Values collegiality
Prophetic woman of prayer and compassion
Kind; Fair
Humble
Inclusive
Patience
A sense of the ridiculous
Negotiating skills
Sensitive to those who hold no position
Meet the needs of people and be willing to speak out
Awareness of our problems
Willingness to speak to authorities

CHAPTER 28
Chicago Catholic Women Celebrates 25 Years

Francis George, O.M.I., was appointed Archbishop of Chicago by the Pope on April 8, 1997. He was made a Cardinal on February 21, 1998. Chicago Catholic Women wrote a letter to him on April 9, 1997, stating that "we look forward to working with him on women's issues" and that "we will appreciate the time you might have to meet with us." We never heard from him.

— ❀❀❀ —

On Thursday, March 19, 1998, Chicago Catholic Women sponsored an evening with Kaye Ashe in conjunction with the Department of Religious Studies-Pastoral Ministry Institute and the Women's Studies Program at St. Xavier University. Kaye spoke about her new book, *The Feminization of the Church?*, which explores the extent and nature of this feminization and how it affects women and spirituality, language, ethics, ministry, and leadership, and how this feminization is affecting the life and future of the Church itself.

— ❀❀❀ —

In 1998 and 1999, we began celebrating liturgies on Pentecost Sunday at A Woman's Place Resource Center in downtown Chicago. On Pentecost Sunday, May 23, 1999, we celebrated a memorial honoring those who had gone before us. Mary Ellen O'Grady helped with the Liturgy and Michelle White danced. We remembered especially: Monica Brown, Mary O'Keefe, Ginny Williams, Carol Zientek, Lana Hostettler, Grace Mary Stern, Penny Severns, Joyce Quinn, and Mary Margaret Johanning. Those who came to the Celebration remembered loved ones and told stories about them.

CCW also began offering Celebrating Cards and Remembering Cards, cards that could be sent for birthdays and other occasions or to remember a loved one who died. There was a note inside that said "A donation has been made in your name to Chicago Catholic Women's Program for Shelter Women."

— ❀❀❀ —

A new group of young women called Young Feminist Network of the Women's Ordination Conference got together for a weekend, September 18–20, 1998, and invited me to speak, giving the history and significance of specific happenings on our journey.

— ❀❀❀ —

On October 24, 1998, Chicago Catholic Women had a liturgy and discussion at St. Xavier University. We invited Jane Higgins, former Assistant Executive Director of Cook County

Jail and warden of Dwight Prison for Women, and Terrie Mc-Dermott, Special Assistant to the Cook County Sheriff and Director for the Intermediate Sanction Project for Women, to speak about their work with women in prison.

— ✽✽✽ —

Later that October, we also began a Companion Program for the shelter women in our Job-Training Program. CCW members volunteered to call graduates of our program to see how they were getting along at their jobs and how well their children were doing.

— ✽✽✽ —

Our Christmas Luncheon Fundraisers in 1997, 1998, and 1999 were held at the Oak Lawn Hilton. This was a bigger facility. In 1997 we again invited Kathy O'Malley and Judy Markey of WGN-Talk Radio and gave an award to the Visiting Nurses Association. Every woman present received an award magnet reading: "To a Remarkable Woman."

Our luncheon in 1998 was held on December 4 and featured a shortened version of the comedy play *Late Nite Catechism*. We honored Mary Kay Flanagan and Ruth Woodring for their courageous stand against the U.S. Army School of the Americas (they were both arrested at the most recent protest and had spent the last six months in prison rather than be silenced); Dolores Brooks for her lifetime effort working for women's equality in Church and in Society; and Barbara Flynn Currie, Majority Leader of the Illinois State House of Representatives, for her continued work for women and children, particularly on issues of choice, child care, and domestic violence.

One of our largest Christmas luncheon crowds ever came to celebrate Chicago Catholic Women's 25th Anniversary on Saturday, December 4, 1999. We honored those who had gone before us and those who were currently present in Chicago Catholic Women. We were fortunate to book the Second City Players, who gave us many laughs.

That was our third year at the Oak Lawn Hilton and not only did we fill the Grand Ballroom for our luncheon, but we also used the adjoining room for groups who wanted to sell their art work, books, and crafts. We usually had twelve tables in that adjoining room and many buyers. For several years, Pat Klein made favors for everyone who came to the luncheon. South Side women who helped to make these programs possible were Mary Lou Beck, Cona Evans, Angie Weiss, Deb Beck, Anna Marie Franko, Patty Gleason, Pat Niego, Ruth Pauly, Kay Philpott, Ginger Krabbe, Ruth Vaulman, Mary Lou Sullivan, Joan Montemurro, Margot Tunney, Dee Pospishil, Mary Ahern, Laurel Kruizenga, Kitty Kelly, Pat Taylor, Dolores Stewart, Sharon Peterson, Donna Kennedy, Eileen Fitzy Tucker, Rose Ann Mulhern, Eileen Heelan, Colette Dupont, Pat Brogan, and Barbara Fiedler.

—❀❀❀—

Chicago Catholic Women decided to make the archives at the Gannon Center for Women and Leadership at Loyola University the home for our records. Material was organized and boxes were packed for several years and received by Carolyn Farrell and Valerie Brown at the Gannon Center. They have been most helpful and, looking back, this was a good decision for Chicago Catholic Women.

We had worked for 25 years—from October 1974 to December 1999. It was time to formally close the story of Chicago Catholic Women and its role in founding the Catholic Women's Movement. The Board of Chicago Catholic Women met and we dissolved the organization.

This I saw as a courageous and radical move. Often, we want to keep something going—whatever the something might be. What we were saying was *We did a good job, and now it is time after 25 years to put a closure to this great work we did as Chicago Catholic Women.* We are different people now at the closing than we were in the beginning. We have learned much and perhaps it is this wisdom and passion that gives us the strength to move on.

In May 2000, I sent the following letter to Chicago Catholic Women:

> Dear Friend of Chicago Catholic Women,
>   They say that one thing in this life that is certain is change. This letter is sent to you to let you know that we are dissolving Chicago Catholic Women. We have had a

great 25 years and the image is one of Mary Tyler Moore throwing her hat in the air, knowing that we are going out on a high note. One response from a person who came with his three children to our Mother's Day witness every year on the steps of Holy Name Cathedral was, "We can never dissolve Chicago Catholic Women because it will always be in our hearts."

For 25 years we have faithfully tried to carry out our goal of 'working to promote the full giftedness and personhood of women and a world of justice for all.' We will hopefully pass this on to future generations in this new century. It is good for organizations to have a beginning-middle-closing, and to celebrate the events which take us through the years we are given on Earth.

The Universe is filled with wonder and questions unanswered. One big question that future generations will ask is about the issue of discrimination—gender discrimination. Why does the Catholic Church hold in its policies the violent and immoral practices that say girl babies who grow up to be women are not good enough to preach or to celebrate the Eucharist, only because they are female? Females are offered six sacraments while the other gender may have seven. Why do governments continue to keep women in slavery—ignoring the U.N.'s declaration against discrimination of women? It is no wonder that women have had enough of this violence, and continue to celebrate Eucharist, to celebrate the sacrament they are to the Universe, and to celebrate our lives as we birth new ideas—going where the Spirit leads us.

Our Center began at 22 E. Van Buren and moved to 1307 S. Wabash, 5249 N. Kenmore, and finally 3343 W. 95th Street—so we have been downtown, the North Side, and the South Side. However, our organization has been known not only locally in Chicago, but nationally and internationally as well, as we took our work for women around the globe. You made Chicago Catholic Women what it is. Our herstory now will be brought to the Archives at the Gannon Center for Women and Leadership located at Mundelein/Loyola University in Chicago. Mailings, letters, photos, media releases, tapes of conferences, tapes of news programs, and a history of events will be there for those who come after us.

Thanks to you for the work of these 25 years. Thanks for your generosity, your tenacity, your passion for justice, your courage, your creativity, and your love which you have shown to the Shelter Women in our Job-Training Program, the women at clinics in the city, and to each other as we worked on networking, educational programs, workshops, conferences, and celebrations, filling rooms with laughter, conversation, and prayer.

Thank you, Thank you, Thank YOU!

May you and your families be blessed forever.

Your Sister,

Donna Quinn

CHAPTER 29
Looking Back, Looking Forward: 2000–2015

At 10:15 p.m. on January 22, 2002, there was a great thundering sound not too far away. I had never heard such a loud, booming noise. I called my brother thinking something had exploded in the area. He said it was lightning. It was so different to have rain, thunder, and lightning in January mixed with warmer weather.

The next morning I received the message that Dolores Brooks had died at 10:45 p.m. The skies had created their own announcement with fireworks—a proper welcome for one whose journey for justice would take a new direction.

Margaret Traxler, founder of the National Coalition of American Nuns, followed Dolores the next month, and my own brother the next year. So many great women and men have gone before us. I know our work for justice continues because of the inspiration, hope, and courage they have left us.

—❀❀❀—

I needed this courage when, after escorting women into health clinics for six years, I received a letter in 2005 from the Chicago Diocesan Office for Religious that Cardinal George had been informed of my activities and I was asked to stop. I wrote a letter directly to the Cardinal listing all the necessary health benefits that women received at the clinic in question, including mammograms, cervical screening for cancer, abortions, STDs, AIDS/HIV screening, etc. He wrote back that my presence there was causing scandal to others. (The protestors were Catholicics from surrounding parishes, praying the rosary and shouting vicious names at the women trying to seek help at the clinic and to the *peacekeepers*, as I called the clinic escorts.)

In the end of many talks I decided not to be a peacekeeper at this clinic but would increase my work in organizing for reproductive rights for women. After this I took on the role of coordinating the Religious Coalition for Reproductive Rights-IL and have been on their National Board for the last three years. I am a firm believer that a woman cannot have full autonomy unless she has reproductive autonomy. A woman has moral authority over her body. Men do not have this decision-making authority over women's bodies, and should rather look into ways to continue to respect women as equals.

In 2013 Women-Church Convergence celebrated 30 years, and in Philadelphia during the September 18–20, 2015, weekend, over 500 women and men came together to celebrate the fortieth anniversary of Women's Ordination Conference. We will keep on celebrating and persevering with passion until all women on Earth have equality.

AFTERWORD
Parting Thoughts

The following is an agenda that we continue to work on through our feminist coalitions.

Societal Issues

We are working on policies and practices around the world so that young girls will have the opportunity for an education and health care, and an end to their being kidnapped, raped, and trafficked.

- There must be an end to all forms of violence against women and a reverence for women's reproductive autonomy.
- Women must have equal pay for equal work.
- The U.S. and all nations must sign on to the U. N.'s Convention on the Elimination of Discrimination ag-ainst Women (CEDAW).
- The U.S. must finally pass the Equal Rights Amendment.

Catholic Church Issues

We are working to put an end to the immoral discrimination against women in the Catholic Church. *Women are not given full membership in the Church*:

Membership for men has seven sacraments.

Membership for women has six sacraments and a man must be present for those six.

- **A feminist sacramental system is needed.**

Membership for men gives them the right to vote for the next pope and at synods on policies, practices, and promulgations.

Membership for women currently says we do not have the right to vote in the Church.

- **A new governance by equals is needed.**

Membership for men gives them the protection of Canon Law.

Membership for women currently gives no protection but they can be tried under a law that says they are not equal under this law.

- **A new code of law needs to be written by female and male feminists.**

Membership for men gives them the right to lead at liturgies and interpret scripture through homilies.

Membership for women currently gives them homily rights with the consent of ordained men.

- **A renewed priestly ministry is needed.**

Membership for men gives them first-class privileges regarding their anatomy and creation of children.

Membership for women denies their reproductive autonomy, which includes her right to make moral decisions about her reproductive anatomy. The Vatican and its bishops prohibit family planning and contraception for women, and parenting, adoption, and foster care for same-sex couples.

•**A new Code of Sexual Ethics must be written by feminist women and men.**

Our work is in direct service but even more so in the analysis of the structures that oppress. We do this with the hope that one day we will celebrate governments, societies, cultures, and a Church that will respect women and call every person to share her/his gifts in a world filled with justice, peace, and equality.

Appendix A
Programs Offered by Chicago Catholic Women

From its beginning, Chicago Catholic Women offered programs and presenters for education and networking. If women were planning a program for a parish group or a women's group, they could call our office and ask for one of the following programs.

- Leadership Development—Understanding Structures (Marge Tuite)
- Women in the Priesthood—Perspectives on a Possibility (Patricia Hughes)
- The Role of Women in the Church Today (Teresa Maltby)
- All Together Now (Susan Weeks)
- Dialogue of Sharing and Caring (Valerie Wojciak)
- Reconciliation in the Church: Woman as Sacramental Minister (Jean Kenny)
- Sacramentality of Life-Consciousness Raising (Georgene Wilson)
- Women in the Church in Chicago—Exclusion or Equal Opportunity (Mary Sullivan)
- Mission to the Church in Chicago (Eileen Burke or Lupita Marie Cordero)
- Raising Awareness Among Women of their Potential

(Marilyn Steffel, Joan Scanlon, and Phyllis Spinal)
- St. Elizabeth Seton and Women in the Church Today (Rosalie Noder and Ann Bracken)

Appendix B
Board Members of Chicago Catholic Women

1975

The Steering Committee/first board of Chicago Catholic Women: Ellen Carroll, Carol Crepeau, Terri Grasso, Georgia Mae Horrell, Joan Krebs, Lois McGovern, Mary Lou Mrozynski, Donna Quinn (Executive Director), Mary Sullivan, Marge Tuite, Katherine Ward, and Susan Weeks.

1976

The second CCW Coordinating Committee: Patricia Crowley, Barbara Davidson, Ella Gardner, Teresina Grasso, Georgia Mae Horrell, Patricia Hughes, Donna Moriarty Kennedy, Joan Krebs, Terry Maltby, Lois McGovern, Carolyn Noonan Parmer, Donna Quinn, Maureen Reiff, Marilyn Steffel, Mary Sullivan, and Marjorie Tuite.

1977

CCW Coordinating Committee: Jennifer Artis, Patty Crowley, Bernardine Dehn, Virginia Gorsche, Georgia Mae Horrell, Joan Krebs, Lois McGovern, Carolyn Noonan Parmer, Mary Powers, Donna Quinn (Executive Director), Maureen Reiff, Marilyn Steffel, Mary Sullivan, Marge Tuite, and Valerie Wojciak.

1978

CCW Coordinating Committee: Monica Cahill, Patty Crowley, Petra

Horst, Carol Luczak, Carmelita Madison, Brenda McCarthy, Lois Mc-
Govern, Pam Montagno, Claudette Nolan, Carolyn Noonan Parmer,
Mary Powers, Donna Quinn, Maureen Reiff, Ann Sipko, Rita Ann Te-
ichman, Marilyn Steffel, Marge Tuite, Marilyn Uline, and Valerie Wojciak.

1979–1985

CCW Coordinating Committee Members in this era: Paula Basta, Ann
Benedict, Peg Boivin, Mary Buckley, Kathy Burke, Susan Catania, Pat-
ty Crowley, Sheila Daley, Audrey Denecke, Loraine Doane, Connie
Driscoll, Margaret Dunn, Barbara Ferraro, Vera Fina, Loretta Finnerty,
Marie Flood, Catherine Gallagher, Maureen Gallagher, Donna Goetz,
Carole Hegarty, Suzanne Holland, Mary Jane Jeffries, Elaine LaLonde,
Carol Luczak, Carmelita Madison, Joellen McCarthy, Lois McGovern,
Katie Murphy, Mary Powers, Donna Quinn, Rosemary Radford Ruether,
Maureen Reiff, Kay Scharf, Suzana Schlessinger, Mary Louise Schneid-
wind, Sue Secker, Ann Sipko, Bernie Smierciak, Madalynn Smith, Mari-
lynn Steffel, Marianne Supan, Margaret Traxler, Marge Tuite, Soyla Vil-
licana, Jacquie Wetherholt, Carla Wilde, and Valerie Wojciak.

1986–1987

CCW Coordinating Committee:

- Ann Benedict
- Yvette Bryant—Chair of Stopping Apartheid Committee
- Joanne Cullen—Co-Chair of the Central America
  Committee
- Sheila Daley

- Connie Driscoll—Chair of Finances Committee
- Catherine Gallagher
- Maureen Gallagher—Chair of Mary's Pence Committee
- Geraldine Gorman—Chair of Peace & Disarmament Committee
- Fran Koval—Chair of Scholarships Committee and Chair of Legislative & Reproductive Rights
- Darlene Noesen—Co-Chair of the Central America Committee.
- Lillie Pang—Co-Chair of Pregnant Teens Committee
- Donna Quinn—Chair of Membership
- Beth Rindler—Chair of Liturgy, Ordination, Preaching Committee
- Sue Secker
- Ruby Taylor—Co-Chair of Pregnant Teens Committee
- Margaret Traxler
- Susan Walker—Chair of Lesbian Rights

1988–1993

CCW Coordinating Committee: Karen Allen, Joanne Cullen, Pat Eggert, Anna Marie Franko, Nancy Golbeck, Mary Hill, Judy Ludwig, Therese Lynch, Darlene Noesen, Donna Quinn, and Carol Zientek.

1994–2000

CCW Coordinating Committee: Mary Lou Beck, Anna Marie Franko, Patty Gleason, Pat Niego, Ruth Pauly, Kay Philpott, Donna Quinn, and Ruth Vaulman.

INDEX OF NAMES

In gratitude for all the women who supported CCW and our work for justice in church and society.

ACKNOWLEDGMENTS

Many people have been part of getting this book produced and published.

You, the reader, are very important to its ultimate function.

We all of course need the many women and men who give of their lives to surround the earth with God's love. May they continue to inspire us with the knowledge that women and men are made in God's image.

In the beginning of the writing process, I asked three people to read the manuscript and respond. Thanks to Kaye Ashe, Carolyn DeSwarte Gifford, and Ellen Skerett for that critical help.

Thanks too to Angie Weiss for her generous hours of typing and proofreading, and to Artlynn Photography for taking the author photo.

I am grateful to Sharon Woodhouse, her production team at Conspire Creative, and for distributing the book through her Chicago imprint Lake Claremont Press: A Chicago Joint. Thanks to Todd Petersen for his design.

It certainly takes many willing and capable people to create a book. Their work and encouragement will be fully realized when we have achieved full equality for women on earth. Meanwhile I give thanks for their laughter and love as we work for full equality in church and society for our sons and our daughters of future generations.

About the Author

Donna Quinn is a feminist, activist, scholar, sister, and friend to many. She has worked in direct service, teaching, job-training, fundraising, marketing, giving shelter to women and children, visiting the sick, and grieving with family and friends those who have gone before us.

Donna's passion and energy is felt through her ongoing work to change structures and systems in church and society that continue to oppress women locally, nationally, and globally. She does this coordinating the National Coalition of American Nuns (NCAN), through her work with the Religious Coalition for Reproductive Choice-IL, and with Women-Church Convergence, a coalition of feminist women and men working through 26 organizations. She firmly believes that women must have reproductive autonomy to achieve full autonomy.